Read what businesspeople like you say about Andy Blackstone...

"... his insights, experience and mentorship have been a key element in our evolution from a small startup company with '2 guys and an idea' to a going concern with 8 employees and a consistently growing top line."
—Kevin Kelly, President, Application Experts

"Andy built a consistent, scalable sales process based on a new value proposition . . . , replacing a bottom-up sales approach that often resulted in significant discounting and contract negotiation with an approach that established the value of our services, all but eliminated contract changes, and maintained list prices in most new client opportunities."
—Vane Clayton, CEO, KPA

"The process of taking a smaller early stage company from the early adopter market phase to more widespread market adoption has unique challenges, and I believe that Andy Blackstone is uniquely qualified to help companies at this stage take the steps required to make that leap."
—Stephen Collins, President, Anark Corporation

"I'm writing to thank you for the positive results that you have delivered to two of our portfolio companies. . . . In both cases, your work in redesigning sales process and in re-orienting the sales effort away from their product focus to a customer focus resulted in increased sales and shorter sales cycles."
—David Billstrom, formerly Managing Partner, FBR Comotion Venture Capital

small changes

That Help Small Companies Make BIG Increases in Sales

ANDY BLACKSTONE

Blackstone Associates Publishing
Lake Oswego, Oregon

Blackstone associates

Blackstone Associates Publishing
510 5th Street
Lake Oswego, OR 97034
www.blackstoneassoc.com
www.smallchangesbook.com

Copyright © 2010 by Andrew J. Blackstone
All rights reserved. No part of this book may be reproduced or transmitted in any form or by any means, electronic or mechanical, including photocopying, recording or by any information storage and retrieval system, without written permission from the author, except for the inclusion of brief quotations in a review.
Published 2010
Printed in the United States of America

ISBN: 978-0-9827311-2-3
Library of Congress Control Number: 2010907543

While every precaution has been taken in the preparation of this book, the publisher and author assume no responsibility for errors or omissions, or for damages resulting from the use of the information contained herein.

SPIN® is a registered trademark of Huthwaite, Inc.
European SPIN® trademarks are held by Huthwaite, Ltd.
Cover photo by Jupiter Images/Getty Images
Design by Jennifer Omner, ALL Publications

Contents

Introduction: Small Changes Make Big Differences — 9
Introducing real people with challenges like yours. 10
Who will benefit the most from reading this book 11
What you can expect to get out of the book. 11
What you'll find in the book 13
Why should I listen to this guy? 15

Part I: Small Changes in Focus — 17
Chapter 1: How to Focus on Your Customer — 19
You know you have a great idea, but sales are a struggle. . . .19
Your focus on your product is causing the problem 21
The small change in focus:
Learning to focus on your customer 23
What the change in focus means to how you sell 29
Case Study:
Construction Systems focuses on its customer. 30
Summary 34

Chapter 2: How to Focus on Your Strengths — 35
Why don't I close more of the deals I go after?. 35
You might be chasing the wrong deals 37
The small change in focus:
Learning to focus on your strengths 38

How the change in focus makes you more effective 42
Case Study: Equity CRM tightens its market focus 43
Summary 45

Chapter 3: How to Focus on Your Value   **47**
Sales aren't bad—why am I not making more money? 47
You're not pricing to take
advantage of the value you're providing 48
The small change in focus:
Learning to focus on your value 50
How the change in focus
helps you generate more profits. 53
Case Study:
Johnson Environmental Services focuses on value 54
Summary 56

Part II: Small Changes in Process   **59**

Chapter 4: How to Identify Your "Ideal Prospect"   **61**
Changing focus is harder than it looks 61
You need to add processes to your focus changes. 62
The small change in process:
Learning to identify your Ideal Prospect 62
How the change in process increases your sales 76
Case Study:
Johnson Environmental Services Finds Its Ideal Prospect . . 76
Summary 78

Chapter 5: How to Build Your Sales Process   **79**
OK, I scheduled the meeting . . . now what? 79
Your sales calls still aren't consistently successful 80
The Small Change in Process:
Building your sales process 82

Contents 7

    How the small change in process puts you in charge 92
    Case Study: Equity CRM builds a sales process 93
    Summary 96

Part III: Managing the Changes   99
Chapter 6:
How to Use Sales Tactics to Implement Your Process   101
    Sales tactics: partnerships, not manipulation 101
    The Secret? Don't pitch products, ask questions 102
    How to ask your questions: a short version of *SPIN*® . . . 104
    How to present your solution 107
    Five fundamental rules for asking questions. 107
    How to plan your sales calls 109
    What will happen as you implement your sales process. . . 112
    Case Study:
    Construction Systems implements its sales process. 113
    Summary 114

Chapter 7: How to Measure, Track and Manage   117
    Setting goals for sales 117
    Automating the process:
    Measuring and tracking sales goals and objectives 124
    Setting up your CRM System 127
    Rolling out your CRM system 128
    Managing sales using the CRM system 129
    What will happen as you track
    and measure your sales process? 130
    Summary 130

Chapter 8: How to Hire and Compensate Salespeople   131
    Hiring challenges. 131
    The successful hiring process 133

Sales Compensation 142
What will happen when you
hire and compensate systematically. 144
Summary 145

Part IV: Closing Thoughts and Some Resources   147
Chapter 9: Closing Thoughts   149
Chapter 10: Resources   153
Selected Books 153
Selected Blogs 154
You Can Help   156
About the Author   157
About the Cover   158

Introduction

Small Changes Make Big Differences

According to the Small Business Administration, only about half of new small businesses are still in business after four years. "Lack of experience" is one of the major factors blamed for this, but the SBA doesn't specify what experience the founders of the unsuccessful businesses are lacking. Practical sales experience I've gained from working with the CEOs of many small companies has revealed founders who have ingenious product ideas and organizational abilities derived from engineering and manufacturing backgrounds, but limited sales experience. I'm convinced this lack of sales experience is a major factor in small business failure. These business founders can often make a go of it for a while with a good product idea and stubborn persistence, but at some point, a professionally designed sales approach is fundamental to creating long-term business growth. A company that does not grow cannot survive.

This book is about a set of small but fundamental changes that can have profound effects on sales success for small companies. I will begin by introducing you to two companies that were struggling with sales challenges and effectively adopted some of these small changes.

Introducing real people with challenges like yours
James Johnson, Johnson Environmental Services

Johnson Environmental Services provides environmental, health, and safety (EHS) consulting and outsourced compliance services to manufacturing companies. It's a healthy, thriving business with 16 employees, and James Johnson, who founded the company 10 years ago and owns and runs it today, is justly proud of what he's accomplished. But James isn't satisfied with where the company is today—he wants to continue its growth and isn't sure how he might accomplish that. He's been very good at retaining current customers and selling them new services, but bringing new customers into the fold has become a major challenge. Part of his problem is that attending to company management tasks just doesn't leave him the time to dedicate to pursuing new customers. Another part of the problem is that James is a college-educated engineer, not a salesman, and he isn't sure what to do to increase his new customer sales. When I met James, he was trying to decide whether to hire a salesperson, outsource sales prospecting to another company, hire a manufacturer's representative firm, or hire an operations manager to take over some management tasks so he could devote more time to sales. All of these possible paths required investments that James was reluctant to make without some assurance of success.

Don Smithers, Construction Systems

Construction Systems provides hand-held computing products for tracking timesheets and progress on large construction projects. This is an interesting technology that offers customers an opportunity to save significant money while helping them manage projects more effectively. Don Smithers, the CEO (and also a major investor in the company) was convinced that the company's success with several major highway construction firms could be leveraged into market domination. However, when he contacted me, the company had not closed a new customer order in six months. They were able to generate high levels of interest in the product, but at the end of a long sales cycle were not able to close the order. Don was frustrated and was trying to decide whether he should fire his sales manager, modify the product, or maybe just shut the company down.

Who will benefit the most from reading this book

This book will provide significant help with sales challenges for most owners, general managers, and sales managers in small businesses. It is important to note that I wrote this book specifically for business owners and managers like James and Don, who manage companies that sell products or services to other companies. Their products and services help their customers improve their businesses, increase their sales, and become more efficient and effective. James and Don each faced a challenge in selling to new customers and expanding his business and both were uncertain about how to solve that problem. Each of them felt the future of his company depended on getting the right answer on the first try. I will revisit both of these executives, and a few other clients I've helped, many times in the course of this book. I'll show you how they overcame these challenges by making small changes in how they approached the way they think about selling and the way they sell.

What you can expect to get out of the book

The purpose of this book is to show you how to significantly expand your sales. You'll profit from reading it if you can relate to any of these scenarios:

- You are a founder/owner/operator of a business that is facing

sales challenges and you just don't have the time to spend on sales—and don't have anyone else you can trust to delegate it to.
- You are considering hiring salespeople or outsourcing your sales and you are unsure of how to proceed to ensure success. One symptom of this is that you aren't sure exactly what you want a new salesperson to do or how you would manage her.
- You've made several unsuccessful attempts to expand sales. You might have hired salespeople who didn't work out, or tried direct mail, or had existing employees make cold calls, or built a new website—all to no avail.
- You have unpredictable sales, with good months and bad months—and you can never see either one coming. You're not sure whether you are going to close a deal until it actually closes, and you lose deals you think you should have won.
- You already have a sales force, and some of the salespeople are stars, but some are not doing well, and you're not sure what makes the difference. You know you should fire the under-performers and find some new stars, but you're not sure how to tell whether you've found a star until long after you've invested in the new hire.

These are really difficult situations, and I understand it's tough to see your way out of them without some major dislocations in the way you do business.

I have good news for you.

> *Small changes in the way you think about and manage your sales efforts can result in large increases in sales and margins.*

Introduction

What I will do is help you understand what needs to change and show you how to make those changes. The changes are small but fundamental, and they are sometimes challenging to implement. None of these changes is rocket science or black magic, however, and each of you will be able to make them in your business. In this book, I'll show you how—one step at a time. As you make the changes that apply to your situation, you'll begin to see the difference very quickly. At Construction Systems, Don Smithers' vice president of sales closed four major deals within two months after they made a few of these small changes. You will begin to be able to manage the sales function just as systematically as you manage the rest of your company. You'll start to realize the full potential of your business and reap the true rewards of the time and energy you've invested over the years.

What you'll find in the book

Three major ideas form the first three parts of the book. Each of these major ideas is broken down into chapters about the small changes that will cause the big sales results. Not all of these changes are needed in every company—you'll pick the ones that apply to you—but all of them warrant serious thought on your part and are worth considering.

The first two parts are about changing how you think about selling and how you can organize yourself to be more effective and efficient as you sell. You may see these parts as more theoretical than practical, but bear with me: Part 3 will give you the nuts and bolts of how you actually implement these changes.

Part I : Small Changes in Focus

I've found that most small company sales challenges occur because company management is focusing on the wrong things. Changing

focus often results in quick and exciting increases in sales. So I begin the book with a section on changing your focus in three ways:
- How you look at the relationship between your product or service and your customers.
- How you look at your markets and customer types.
- How you look at your pricing, your margins, and the value you bring to your customer.

Part II: Small Changes in Process
Once you've changed your focus, you'll need to organize your business to be both effective and efficient at selling. This section deals with changes in your business processes that will help you sell in a more organized way:
- How you define and prospect for your "ideal customer."
- How you organize the way you pursue sales opportunities.
- How you conduct your day-to-day selling.

Part III: Managing the Changes
Finally, you are going to have to implement these changes in focus and process in the real world, which will require a set of small changes in the way you manage your sales effort. This section deals with how you manage your sales force and your sales opportunities:
- How you measure and monitor your sales and your salespeople.
- How you set goals and track sales variables.
- What tools you use to implement your measurement and tracking.
- How you hire and compensate your salespeople.
- How you train and mentor your salespeople.

Part IV: Closing Thoughts and Some Resources
This section provides some closing thoughts and recommendations, along with some additional resources that may be helpful.

Why should I listen to this guy?
I've spent more than 35 years as a salesperson, sales manager, and vice president of sales, selling business-to-business products and services. I've also been a small-business owner, confronting the problems I'll discuss in this book. I've believed for a long time that consistent process, not black magic, is the secret to sales success. In the past 10 years or so, my clients have taught me that it isn't big reorganization or re-engineering that is most valuable to them—it's the small changes that have big results that really matter. This book is the outcome of the lessons they've taught me as we've worked together to improve their sales, their margins, and their lives.

Part I

Small Changes in Focus

Chapter 1

How to Focus on Your Customer

You know you have a great idea, but sales are a struggle
You probably started your company with an idea—an idea for a product or a service that you thought other companies would buy to improve their businesses (for the sake of simplicity, from now on when I talk about products, I'm including services). You worked hard, and your idea actually became a product you could sell. You presented this product to a lot of potential customers, and a few of them bought it from you. You persisted, improved the product, sold it to more customers, and built a successful business. It was hard work. For a lot of you, it keeps on being hard work. You thought that as you acquired more customers, things would get easier, but they haven't. Closing a deal often is still a battle, you aren't able to price the product higher to increase your margins, and the company hasn't really taken off in the way you thought it would. You've built a nice business, but it hasn't brought the returns or the peace of mind you envisioned.

You're no different from a lot of other small-business owners who had great ideas and turned them into products, only to discover that selling those products wasn't nearly as easy as they thought it would be. The difficulty often comes from a relentless focus on your product—a natural focus for small businesses. I've worked with businesses where the benefits of their product were so evident it looked like they had a license to steal, but they were still encountering serious sales challenges.

Small company founders, owners, or managers like you who have turned ideas into products are rightfully convinced that your product is absolutely necessary to a prospect's success and that buying it is the obvious thing for your prospects to do. This leads to the belief (conscious or unconscious) that the product is so good it sells itself. You just know that the prospect needs what you are selling, even if the prospect doesn't realize it. You are convinced that if you pitch the product hard enough, explain it often enough, and are persistent enough, the prospect just has to buy. So you spend your time pitching the features and the benefits of your product. You may have put together a slick PowerPoint presentation or a great demonstration of your product. You can tell your prospect exactly how the product will save him money or increase his sales. You have references from customers who are a lot like this prospect. *And the prospect still doesn't buy.*

Several bad things are happening here.

- **First**, you don't get an order.
- **Second**, you are apt to dismiss those prospects who don't buy as people who "just don't get it" and are not savvy enough to understand the obvious benefits of buying the product. It's even more confusing because a lot of those prospects who don't buy seem to be very interested in what you're selling. That, of course, motivates you to spend more time with them—time that is wasted when they ultimately decide not to buy.

- And **finally**, the time you spend on these prospects makes it very difficult for you to manage your selling time effectively, which has a negative impact on your ability to sell to those prospects who do "get it."

The trap in selling this way is that you are successful just often enough to make you think your approach is working. There are enough prospects who do "get it" to keep business coming in. Psychologists call this "intermittent reinforcement," and its effect is incredibly strong. It makes you think you are focused on your customer, when what you are really focused on is your own vision of what the customer needs. Unfortunately, you end up selling to a fraction of your potential market, and you leave a lot of business on the table. Think about this: What if you could reach those prospects that don't "get it" and make them into customers? What if you could start closing those deals that you are losing because you somehow can't convince a prospect to buy? If you can deal with these "what ifs," you can achieve a significant lift in your sales without a matching increase in the effort you are putting in.

The good news is that you *can* sell to these prospects. I'll show you how in this chapter, but first you need to understand what is causing the problem.

Your focus on your product is causing the problem

The overriding reason that prospects don't buy, even when they seem very interested, is your focus on selling your product. You are offering a solution to them when they don't yet think they have a problem. What you are selling may be very interesting to them. They may be very attentive as you present and demonstrate your product. They may even ask for more information. After all, they are running a business and want to understand what is new and different in their industry or market. But they do not see you as helping them solve a problem that is critical to their business success or as helping them accomplish an important business goal.

It's instructive to think about your own reactions to someone who is trying to sell you some product or service to improve your business. If you are genuinely interested in what's being pitched, you may look like a real prospect to that seller, even though you have no intention of buying—after all, you don't have a problem like the one he can solve. His story is interesting, but not compelling.

That is the difference between selling something that is essential to the success of your prospect's business and selling something that is interesting and might be "nice to have." The only prospects who are buying from you are those who already recognize they have a serious problem that you can solve. The interesting thing is that they will recognize this as soon as you describe the product to them, and you will have an easy sale, not because you are doing a great job of selling, but because they know they have a real problem to solve. And the prospects who don't "get it" are not going to buy, no matter how hard you pitch your product, because they don't think they have a problem that needs solving. Your product pitch only works on prospects who realize they have a problem before you even show up. So, you are missing lots of sales where prospects have a problem you can solve but don't recognize it. This can be immensely frustrating and financially difficult for you.

The lesson is that there is no solution without a problem.

Too often, selling the features and benefits of a product makes it look like a solution *in search* of a problem rather than a solution *to* a problem. Fortunately, there is a better way to sell. It begins by moving your selling focus from your product to your customer's problem.

The small change in focus:
Learning to focus on your customer

The change in focus that you must make to overcome these challenges is to begin thinking about your customer as you sell, rather than about your product. You don't have to change your focus very much to have a quick and significant effect on your sales. To make the change, you must start thinking about sales from the customer's point of view, rather than from yours. This requires a fundamental change in your thinking, but it isn't particularly complicated. Here are three steps to get you started:

- **First,** you must begin thinking about the features and benefits of your product in terms of the critical problems you are solving for your current customers. You have to figure out which problems your prospects and customers think are important, and then figure out which of your product features will provide the solution to those problems. Be careful—it's very easy for you to think about problems you can solve and then pick the ones that you think your prospects and customers *should* think are important, rather than the ones they actually *do* think are important. The following exercise will help you focus on the real problems they have, rather than the ones you would like them to have:

    Begin by thinking about why your current customers bought the product from you. When you think you have the answer, check it out by asking those customers why they bought and what problem they were worried about when you showed up with a solution. Probe deeply for the real reasons they bought, and be sure you understand the nuances and details of the problem they solved with your product. To get at the important real reasons for their purchase, you might try to understand what your customers were trying to accomplish, rather than focusing on the problem they were solving. Pay particular attention to how they are using your product. Ask yourself if it is the way you intended it would be used. Are they creatively making a different use of the product from what you thought they would? What product features are important to them?

Now go to Figure 1.1 and fill out the first three rows. Begin by listing what your customer is trying to accomplish and what problems are keeping her from accomplishing that goal. Then list the features of your product that have helped her solve these problems and accomplish her goal. Figure 1.2 has an example developed by Don Smithers at Construction Systems that should help you as you fill out Figure 1.1.

When you have completed this exercise, you have started to change the way you approach your prospects. You understand the prospect's point of view, and how it might link back to the features of your products. You are changing your focus from your product to your customer. It's not an accident that product features are in the third row of the table, after the list of accomplishments and problems—that's where they rank in their importance to your sales success. As I promised in the introduction, in Part III, I'll talk about the tactics for using this information to increase your sales.

What Customer is Trying to Accomplish	Problems that are Blocking Accomplishment	Product Features that Solve the Problems	"Hair on Fire" Job Function	Possible Titles of Initial Contact

Figure 1.1: Accomplishments, Problems, Features, and Contacts

What Customer is Trying to Accomplish	Making foremen and supervisors more productive by reducing their paperwork and providing daily feedback on project progress.
Problems that are Blocking Accomplishment	1. Projects are widespread and don't have access to central computer. 2. Foremen must write down employee, time, and safety information every day, which takes an hour of unproductive time. 3. Foremen must drive to lockbox to drop off timesheet information daily, which takes as much as an hour. 4. All handwritten data must be manually entered into the computer system. 5. Progress reports can only be delivered on a weekly basis, which keeps foremen from taking quick action to increase productivity or correct problems.
Product Features that Solve the Problems	1. Handheld computers bring computing power to the worksite. 2. Prepackaged menus allow quick data entry with stylus. 3. Data gets uploaded over any dial-up connection, eliminating the foreman's drive and the data entry problem while increasing accuracy. 4. Intermediate server software provides daily updates of project progress to the handheld device.
"Hair on Fire" Job Function	1. The person that is responsible for job performance on a project. 2. The person that is responsible for company financial performance and overall productivity.
Possible Titles of Initial Contact	1. VP Operations 2. CFO

Figure 1.2: Accomplishments, Problems, Features, and Contacts—Construction Systems Example

- **Second**, now that you understand the problem you can solve for your prospect's company, you must determine specifically who you are going to sell to. You must identify the person—or people—who are likely to be experiencing the problem you can solve. The best way to think about this is to first figure out what job function would be likely to encounter this problem. For example, you might say, "a person who makes sure the company never ships a defective product." Once you've done that, you can think about what that person's title might be, or what department they would be working for. In our example, the person might be a quality control engineer working in manufacturing.

   This person will be trying to accomplish an outcome or result that your product can help her achieve and will be struggling with challenges as she tries to achieve the result. She will be looking for ways to overcome these challenges. A good question to ask yourself is, "Whose hair is on fire?" This will be someone who will be absolutely focused on putting out the fire. Go back to Figure 1.1 and fill in the last two rows with possible job functions and titles. Again, the example in Figure 1.2 will help you see how to do this. If you've identified her correctly, when you contact her, you can easily start a productive conversation by asking her how she is dealing with the problem. In Chapter 6, I'll talk about tactics you can use to accomplish this.

- **Third**, you must quantify the financial effect on the prospect if the problem is not solved. As I said, there is no solution without a problem. There is also no solution if failing to solve the problem isn't costing the prospect some significant amount. It's your job to help your prospect figure out what that number is. This is different from coming up with an imaginary return on investment (ROI) based on some average case that you have either made up or derived from the experience of your current customers. The prospect will not believe any ROI number that you present to her—and she shouldn't believe it, because it may not reflect her specific business challenges at all. This is another point at which presenting and demonstrating without understanding the specific prospect's issues will have no good effect and will not result in an order—it may even destroy your credibility with your prospect.

So you must think through what the implications of not solving the problem might be for your prospect. What might happen if the problem continues, and what kind of costs might be associated with that? It's time to go back to your current customers and explore this with them. Find out what cost implications led them to buy your solution. Probe deeply again, because some of these costs will be subtle, and others may not be in the department that bought the product. Remember, you're not trying to build a case to present to a prospect; you're trying to understand what the elements of cost might be so you can ask your prospect about the impact they have on her.

So now you're ready to change your focus from your product to your prospect. You understand the critical problems your prospect is likely to have that you can help solve. You know who you need to contact to begin your sales effort. And you have some ideas about how to help that person justify the purchase of your product. It's time to talk about how you actually implement this change in focus.

How to Focus on Your Customer

What the change in focus means to how you sell

I'm going to discuss sales tactics in some detail in Part III. What I'll do here is take a long view of how this change in focus will change the way you sell and the results you will achieve.

The biggest change in your selling will be that you will stop making sales presentations and doing product demonstrations early in your sales cycle, before you understand what is going on with your prospect. Instead, you will be asking a lot of questions about the prospect's company, the problems it is encountering, the financial implications of the problems, what your contact is already doing about them, and what else he needs to do about them. You'll be asking, not presenting. You'll be listening, not pitching. You will be sitting on the same side of the table as your contact, helping him define his problem and its possible solutions, giving him insight into what's possible, and helping him build the financial case for buying from you.

Three essential agreements—plus a fourth

You must arrive at three essential agreements with your prospect before you present or demonstrate your product in any more than a very cursory way. These agreements will be meaningless if you don't arrive at them with the person who is able to commit to a purchase of your product. Your new focus will lead naturally to forging these agreements.

- **First**, an agreement with the prospect that he has a problem that is important enough to need an immediate solution, because he has a goal to accomplish that is being blocked by the problem.
- **Second**, an agreement with the prospect that not solving this problem has associated costs large enough to justify paying for a solution.

- **Third**, an agreement that a solution or solutions that would solve the problem might be available.

When you have arrived at these three agreements, you have established that there is a problem worth solving, that it is expensive not to solve it, and that solutions are available. It is finally time to talk about, present, and demonstrate your product as one solution that will solve the prospect's problem, allow him to accomplish his goal, and deliver the financial benefits he has agreed are achievable.

That will lead to the **fourth** agreement—an agreement that your product provides an acceptable solution to the problem.

Let's go back to our initial premise that only the prospects that "get it" are buying. In this environment, your toughest competition is people who are "getting by" by doing what they are doing, and who don't recognize the problem. With this change in focus, you have the opportunity to transform a prospect who might not have been aware of his problem or its costs into a prospect who "gets it" and is now much more likely to buy your product. You've expanded your market, and you haven't spent any more time or effort than you would have when you were selling the old way. You are gaining the large effect from the small change.

Case Study:
Construction Systems focuses on its customer

I'm going to use Construction Systems as an example of this change. In spite of having a solution that its executives were absolutely sure solved a critical problem for their prospects, in spite of having developed a sophisticated ROI analysis for the construction industry, in spite of having several very good reference accounts, they hadn't sold a solution to a new customer for six months.

They thought they had a "license to steal," but they weren't able to consistently sell their product. Here's what they did and what happened.

CEO Don Smithers and I, along with Pete Jackson, the VP of Sales and the only salesperson, decided that they needed to know what the difference was between their current customers and the prospects who hadn't bought, because Don and Pete had thought their sales approach was identical for both groups. They first interviewed the VPs of Operations for three of their current satisfied customers. In each case, the VP of Operations was in charge of using the product and had been an important part of the decision to buy. They asked the VPs why they bought the product, what the benefits were now that the software had been installed and was in use, and how they had made the initial decision to buy.

Don and Pete found out that in each case, the customer had been trying to accomplish a goal of increased productivity on its construction projects—and was encountering a problem that had to do with the difficulty of keeping paper records on jobs that were a considerable distance from the home office. These records were input into the computer system that tracked progress on the job, provided hours worked to the payroll system, and generally provided the numbers needed to manage the company. When Construction Systems showed up pitching a product designed to solve this problem, these companies had already recognized their problem and were ready to buy a solution. They were open about the problem and what it cost, and were very helpful in defining an acceptable solution. All that was required was to convince them that the product could, in fact, solve the problem, which Construction Systems was able to do. They also found out that in each case, the CEO of the company was very involved, first in the definition of a problem needing to be solved and then in the evaluation of whether the product would provide a solution.

We then reviewed all the deals that Construction Systems had lost over the past six months to see if we could find a pattern. And we did. The first thing that stood out is that Don and Pete were doing demonstrations over the Web on the first or second sales call to try to convince the contact that he should investigate buying the product. They felt they had to do this because the person they were talking to didn't see the problem—so they were using the demo to show him how good things could be. There was intense interest, but no recognized problem to solve. The second common factor was that the initial selling was to a mid-level manager who would not allow the salesperson access to upper management and the CEO. If a contact actually figured out that he wanted the product, what followed was a series of sales calls, presentations, and demonstrations to various people in the prospect company, which led to development of a final proposal and pricing. This proposal was then presented to the prospect's upper management and CEO, who were seeing it for the first time. Predictably, their focus was on the price of the solution, not on the problem being solved, and they quickly made a decision not to buy.

So Construction Systems made a series of small changes. Don and Pete developed a 13-step sales process that they divided into three phases:

- The first phase included seven steps which established the first three agreements with the CEO of the prospect company.
- The second phase included four steps: a presentation and demo; gaining the fourth agreement; development and presentation of a proposal; and obtaining a commitment that Construction Systems was the selected vendor.

- The third phase included the final two steps; negotiating and obtaining a contract and beginning implementation of the solution.

The sales process Construction Systems developed can be found in Figure 1.3.

The process was important, and I'll show you how to build one in Chapter 5—but what Construction Systems really changed was

Construction Systems Sales Process Steps

☑	Sales Process Steps	Date Completed
PROSPECT STAGE:		
☐	Prospect CEO contacted and shows interest in Construction Systems.	_____
☐	CEO's agreement obtained about important problem.	_____
☐	CEO's agreement obtained about what he is trying to accomplish.	_____
☐	All prospect influencers and recommenders contacted.	_____
☐	Problem quantified with CEO and other contacts; ROI understood.	_____
☐	CEO's agreement obtained about problem quantification and ROI.	_____
☐	CEO's agreement obtained that solutions are possible.	_____
QUALIFIED STAGE:		
☐	Construction Systems presentation and product demonstration completed.	_____
☐	Construction Systems solution developed, CEO agreement obtained.	_____
☐	Problem and solution verified and approved by all contacts.	_____
☐	Construction Systems proposal developed and formally presented to CEO and other contacts.	_____
☐	Construction Systems formally selected as vendor.	_____
CLOSING STAGE:		
☐	Negotiation of terms and conditions completed; signed contract is obtained.	_____
☐	Implementation is under way.	_____

Figure 1.3: Sales Process Steps

its focus. Don and Pete stopped focusing on presenting the features and benefits of their product, and started focusing on their prospects' problems. They also started working with the only person who could commit the prospect to purchasing the solution—the CEO—and concentrated on arriving at the four essential agreements.

The results were spectacular. In the two months after instituting the small changes, Construction Systems closed four new customers. They were also able to stop working with several prospects where it became obvious that it would not be possible to arrive at the essential agreements with the CEO, which freed up additional time for working on other more qualified prospects.

Summary

You've seen how changing your focus from your product to your prospect's problem can have dramatic and positive sales results. The next change in focus I am going to talk about is a change in the way you think about your marketplace.

Chapter 2

How to Focus on Your Strengths

Now that you're focused on your customer, it's time to talk about your marketplace and how another small change in focus can significantly increase your efficiency and effectiveness as you sell.

Why don't I close more of the deals I go after?

Many, if not most, small businesses are reluctant to turn down any business because of their constant struggle with the need for immediate cash flow. They adopt what I call an "opportunistic" or "shotgun" selling style. Their salespeople call on anyone who could conceivably become a customer, ignore any negative information that would suggest these people are not good prospects, and work very hard at convincing them that the product will provide enough benefit that they should buy it. When one of these prospects buys, the sale often leads to problems that have a negative impact on both revenues and profits. Usually, this is because the solution doesn't quite match the prospective customer's problem.

This selling style can have a negative impact on your revenue and profit in a number of ways:

The low hit rate problem

First, your hit rate on closing business like this is low, because you are not bringing measurable value to your prospective customer. You lose deals to competitors who are providing more value—and you also lose deals because the prospect who doesn't see compelling value often decides to do nothing. So, between the deals you lose and the deals that never happen, your sales efficiency and effectiveness are very low, and your cost of sales is quite high. Your potential revenues are lower than they should be because the number of deals you can do is limited by the number of sales calls you can make—and you are spending those sales calls on deals you don't get. Your sales cycles on deals you get are longer because your prospects are wondering about whether you are delivering value, further limiting your ability to close more deals and generate more revenue.

The customization problem

In order to close a deal, you often kick off the **second** bad effect. In your efforts to create enough value to get the deal, you end up customizing the product for each customer, increasing your cost without achieving an increase in your price. Not only that, you are on a new learning curve for each product delivery, and you aren't building expertise in any solution area, so it doesn't get easier to create value for your next prospect. You get into a vicious cycle where your costs continue to increase and your margins and profits continue to erode.

The differentiation problem

The **third** bad effect is that you make it very difficult to build a market niche where you have differentiation that results in a competitive advantage. You don't have references from customers that resemble your next prospect; you don't have the confidence that comes from successfully delivering to many customers; and you don't have the industry experience that lets you sell the value of your solution. Without differentiation, deals can become competitive dog fights, ending with tough price negotiations. This takes time and energy and strips the profit from the deals you do get. And it makes it very difficult to build a consistent, sustainable, and successful sales operation, because every new prospect becomes an adventure.

I hope I've convinced you that the effort to increase revenues by opportunistically selling to prospective customers who aren't in your "sweet spot" actually is counterproductive, resulting in long sales cycles, low closing rates, high cost of sales, and low margin business. You're working hard, not closing enough deals, and not being as successful as you should be.

You might be chasing the wrong deals

The overriding cause of this problem is that you are not precisely defining and pursuing the market segments and prospective customers that give you the highest probability of success. To succeed in today's incredibly competitive markets, you have to leverage your strengths every way you can. You can't afford not to know exactly who your best prospects are and why, and you can't afford to do business with anyone *but* your best prospects.

If you can't identify your best prospects, you can't concentrate your selling on the companies that have the highest potential to buy. If your salespeople don't know very clearly who and what they are looking for, they have no way to accurately qualify a prospective customer. This means that they will see every prospect they encounter as qualified until that prospect decides not to buy. Since your salespeople don't have the tools to identify unqualified prospects early in the sales cycle, they have no way to become either efficient or effective in their sales efforts.

The attitude that "all business is good business" keeps you from even thinking about how you might improve your situation. I hope the rest of this chapter convinces you that an awful lot of available business is actually bad business, and that it's possible to increase both revenues and profits by limiting the kinds of prospective customers you want to do business with. All it requires is a small change in focus.

The small change in focus: Learning to focus on your strengths

The change in focus you need to make to solve this problem is to start selling only to prospective customers in markets where you can leverage your strengths. Leveraging your strengths is the only way you can establish the value of your solution, build differentiation against your competition, and have control over your pricing and your margins. Like the first change in focus I talked about, this will take some work, but it's still not rocket science and will pay off with big dividends in increased sales and margins.

Three essential steps will help you focus on your strengths:

Identify the "sweet spot"
markets and prospects where you are strongest

First, you must identify the markets and prospective customers where you provide maximum value and have the best references, and

How to Focus on Your Strengths

where your product fits with minimal changes or customizations. Industries and companies like these will be the easiest prospects to sell to, and will also be the easiest to deliver to and satisfy. To do this, begin by going back to the work you did in Chapter 1 and look at it from a different angle. Figure out what kinds of companies and market segments are most likely to have the problems that you can solve and are most likely to understand the value your solution provides. You should consider the following questions as you develop a list of the industry segments and company types you will pursue:

- What are the industry segments where you have the most successful customer relationships? Be as specific as you can; not "Manufacturing Companies," but "Metal Fabricators;" not "Construction Companies," but "Residential Painting Contractors."
- Which customers have realized the best value from purchasing and using your product? Are they similar types of companies? How have they achieved this value, and how do they quantify it? Can you provide and quantify this value for other companies like these?
- Where have you built the most expertise in delivering solutions to your customers' problems? Are they industry-specific? Can you package these solutions and sell them to other companies?
- Which customers would provide you with the best references? What kind of references can you obtain? Letters? Videos? Case studies?
- Where have you built the best competitive advantage for yourself? How can you position your company and product to leverage that advantage with new prospects?

- Are there geographical considerations you need to take into account? What geographic territories can you successfully sell into at a reasonable cost?
- What kinds of customers do you find it easiest to work with? Large customers or small? Public or private?
- What are the specific companies you already know about that fit these criteria?

Answering these questions will help you build a reasonably tight list of potential market segments and companies that you might sell to. More importantly, you will be able to exclude a large number of companies and industry segments where you have a very small likelihood of being successful in your sales efforts.

This initial list will provide some boundary conditions and exclude a large number of companies and industry segments where you have no particular value to offer or competitive advantage you can create. Remember, your goal is to end up with the shortest list that will allow you to meet your sales goals, not the longest list you can think of.

Build a list of prospects to contact

Second, take the work you've just done and get more specific. Build a list of companies that you will target during the next few months. Use any source you can find—some possibilities include Web searches, local business journals' "Book of Lists," referrals from current customers, and industry associations. For each of these companies, figure out who you will initially contact, using your work from Figure 1.1. You now have a prospect list to concentrate on as you sell. The diagram in Figure 2.1 shows how the various factors come together in your list.

How to Focus on Your Strengths

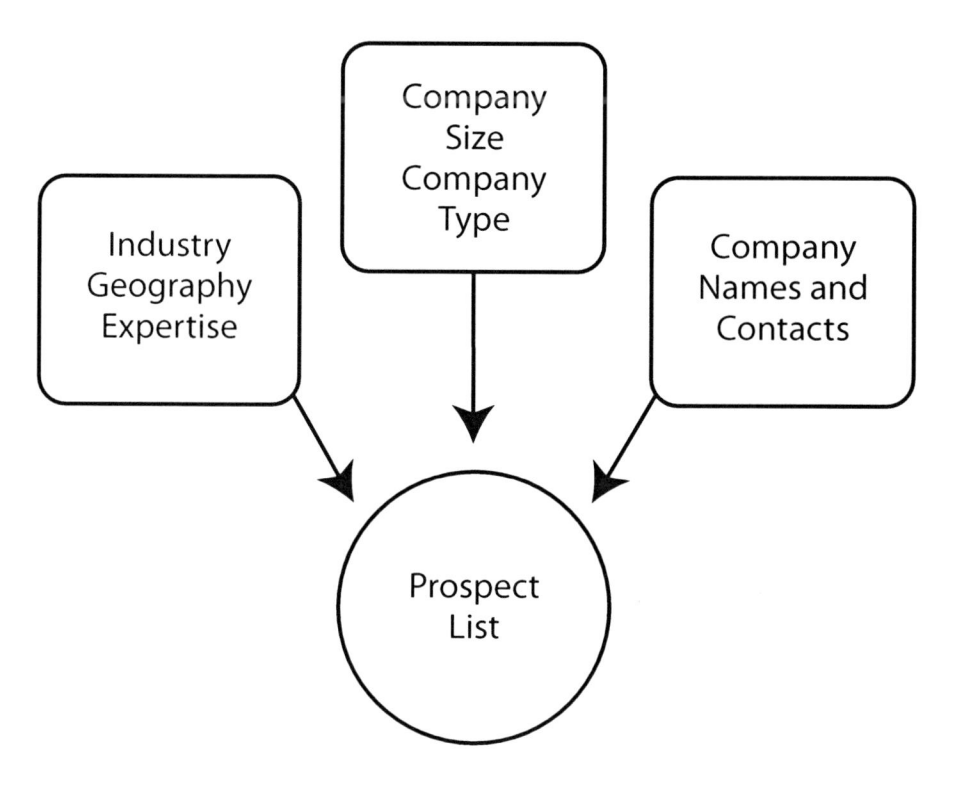

```
   ┌──────────┐
   │ Company  │
   │   Size   │
   │ Company  │
   │   Type   │
   └──────────┘
┌──────────┐  │  ┌──────────┐
│ Industry │  │  │ Company  │
│Geography │  │  │Names and │
│Expertise │  │  │ Contacts │
└──────────┘  ▼  └──────────┘
      ↘  ( Prospect )  ↙
         (   List   )
```

Figure 2.1: Building Your Prospect List

Commit to your strengths

Third, and most importantly, you must commit to concentrating on the industry segments and companies you've defined, and stop selling to everyone else. This is the change in focus that will bring you the big rewards. This takes commitment and patience—and courage. It will mean walking away from deals that you are sure you can get but that don't fit the definition and don't provide the leverage, revenue, and margins that you need. It means working only with prospects where you know you bring value—and understanding how to help them quantify the value.

This doesn't mean that you can't decide to pursue a new market segment as your company grows. It just means that you should go through a process that helps you define exactly what value you expect to bring to that market and how you plan to sell to the companies in the market. What you're trying to do is eliminate "shotgun selling," where you haven't gone through the thinking that assures you of acquiring profitable business from your efforts.

How the change in focus makes you more effective

When you focus on your strengths, you will see a big change in your sales results.

- **First**, you will find that you are *more efficient* in your selling efforts. Things will get easier and less frustrating. You will stop wasting time chasing deals that are never going to happen because you can't deliver value to the prospect; you will shorten the sales cycle on the deals you do pursue, because the value you offer is apparent to these prospects; and you will be spending your selling time working with people who have low resistance to buying from you.
- **Second**, you will be *more effective* in your selling efforts. You will increase your sales without a matching increase in your costs. You will close a higher percentage of the deals you pursue as you begin helping your customers solve their problems and accomplish their goals. Your cost of sales will go down as your salespeople close more deals in each time period. Your revenues will increase, because each salesperson is able to pursue and close more deals.
- **Third**, you will *increase your margins and profits* as you

leverage your expertise, your customer references, and your proven value to justify higher prices for your products. You will eliminate competitors and remove price competition by differentiating your company and your product with the value you provide your customers.

* And **finally**, you will *further increase your margins* as your cost of delivering and installing your product drops because you are no longer doing customizations and you have systematized your product delivery.

So, when you make this focus change, you get more sales, lower cost of sales, higher revenues, better margins, and more efficient deliveries and installations—with no increase in your level of effort or cost of doing business.

Case Study: Equity CRM tightens its market focus

I'd like to introduce you to another client—Roger Spears, the founder and president of Equity CRM. Equity provides customer relationship management solutions for venture capital firms, private equity companies, and endowments. The solutions are built on Web-based software from a company called Salesforce.com, and include both software licenses and consulting and implementation services. The software licenses provide the recurring revenue at low cost that delivers most of the company's profits. When I began working with Roger, the company had several clients in each of its target markets, and had grown to about six people. Roger was still doing almost all of the selling. The problem was that the company was not selling very many software licenses, was doing a lot of consulting, and was not meeting either sales or margin goals. We began by working on Roger's value proposition, but decided the main problem was a little different from what we thought.

When we began looking at where his orders were coming from, two things became obvious. First, a number of prospective customers had been in the sales cycle for months with no progress toward an order, and Roger was continuing to work with them on a weekly basis in an effort to close the deal; and second, many of the consulting engagements that had been providing most of the company's monthly revenue were not connected to the solution Equity CRM had developed—they were basic Salesforce.com consulting work and produced no license revenue. The reason the company was accepting the consulting business was its need for current cash flow to cover expenses.

We looked more carefully at the prospects that were languishing in Equity's sales pipeline and discovered that most of them were venture capital and private equity firms. These companies were impressed with the solution and continued to be interested and ask questions, but could not be persuaded to sign a contract. Equity had not established sufficient value to motivate these customers to buy.

Along with this, we knew that the most recent license deals that had closed were with large university endowments. Given this information, Roger decided the most promising market was the endowment market. He based this decision on a combination of current customer successes, the expertise he had built in providing them with valuable solutions, and their willingness to provide glowing references. He went to work defining his best prospects and building his value proposition. Roger identified 50 endowments that met his criteria.

He made the decision to change focus. He decided to stop pursuing consulting business that was not tied to software licenses, and to aggressively work on contacting and selling to the 50 endowments he identified. He also decided to stop working with the companies in his sales pipeline unless they made a commitment that they were ready to buy.

The results were very satisfying. Roger built a new sales pipeline of endowments and closed two new deals within three months of starting this process—one of them the largest deal his company had ever done. As an additional benefit, he discovered that because he was focusing on the value he brought to a limited set of customers, he was able to stop negotiating his prices and could increase his margins.

Summary

You've worked through two of the three changes in focus.

You have learned to focus on the critical problems you can solve for your prospects and on helping them accomplish their goals, which is helping you to expand your market, sell more efficiently and effectively, and increase your sales.

And, you've begun to focus on your strengths with highly targeted selling and have increased your sales efficiency and effectiveness, reduced your cost of sales, and increased your revenues without increasing your costs. You're ready to consider how you can change focus to increase your margins.

Chapter 3

How to Focus on Your Value

You've come a long way. You know how to focus on solving your prospects' problems and helping them accomplish their goals, rather than focusing on the features and benefits of your product, and you're selling to real prospects with real problems that you can help solve. Now I'll show you how another small change can increase the margins and profits on your sales.

Sales aren't bad—why am I not making more money?

You are probably like most small businesspeople and set your prices based on some combination of your costs, your competitors' prices, and negotiation pressure from your prospects. For those of you selling physical products, this means you are setting prices based on some percentage you add to your costs. You then modify that number as necessary to meet your competition and market conditions. If you have a service business, you will set prices based on some hourly cost plus an added percentage, again modified by competition and market.

Pricing based on your costs creates a large problem for you. It makes it difficult for you to generate sufficient cash flow to expand your business. You tend to get locked into a "just getting by" syndrome, where you are challenged every month to generate adequate revenue to cover your costs. The truth is that you can't generate any financial leverage for your business when your prices are tied directly to your costs.

It's actually worse than that. Once you have set your pricing, it comes under tremendous pressure from competitors—there's always at least one who's trying to buy market share, or who just doesn't understand the problem. Sure, some of these guys will eventually go out of business because they can't make money, but while they are there they are making things very difficult for you. You also open the door to a prospect who negotiates based on arguing about what your costs really are. This kind of prospect feels he must be a tough negotiator to determine what your real price is, creating additional price pressure for you. On top of that, your salesperson often wants to use price as the easy way to close business, and will pressure you to discount your price to get the deal. The combination of these factors makes it very difficult to generate any excess cash for your business.

To sum up, you are limiting your ability to generate margins and profits by not considering what the value of your product or the service you provide to your customer means to your pricing model. Even though the focus changes that you have made mean you're selling more business to better customers, you're still not seeing the monetary benefits you'd like to.

You're not pricing to take advantage of the value you're providing

This problem occurs because you haven't taken advantage of the unique financial value in your solution. You must establish that your solution not only solves a critical problem for your prospect, but that the combination of your company, your product, and your understanding of her industry and business issues brings a unique solution to the table that provides the prospect with a measurable financial benefit. Until you've done this, it's difficult for you to establish that your solution brings more value to the prospect than other solutions she is evaluating.

This lack of differentiation allows the prospect to take the position that the products she is evaluating are commodities, that the only variable that matters is price, and that the most important part of the purchasing process is tough price negotiation. And you can't really blame her, because if she is right and the solutions really aren't that different from one another, then her best strategy is to minimize the price she pays.

As I discussed in Chapter 1, if you are focused on the features and benefits of your product, rather than on solving a critical problem and helping to accomplish important goals, you will find that you generate objections, comparisons to competitors, and tough negotiations based on your price, even if you are the favored supplier.

The really bad part of this is that the prospect focuses on the cost of the solution rather than on its effect. Costs get evaluated against budgets, which mostly are unrelated to the effects of not solving problems. This means your price must fit into a budget that has no relationship to the value you bring. The lesson here is that in order for you to have pricing flexibility, your price must be seen as an investment that has a substantial return, rather than as a cost going against a fixed budget. If you can establish that relationship, you have achieved the ability to price based on that return rather than on your costs.

Let's see how a change in focus can help you move from cost-based to value-based pricing.

The small change in focus:
Learning to focus on your value

The change you must make as you develop your pricing model is to focus on the financial value you are bringing to your prospect, instead of on what it costs you to deliver your solution. This is the way you can position yourself to increase your margins and profits. Like your other focus changes, this is hard work, even though the change itself is fairly simple. Effecting this change in focus requires three steps:

- **First**, think back to the work you did when you were helping your prospect quantify what it would cost if she didn't solve the problem. Take a slightly different slant on the numbers: Use the information about what not solving the problem is costing to figure out what the overall financial effect of your solution will be. You must once again probe into the details and be sure you are not missing any significant financial effect your solution will bring. You also should think about the effect of time. Do the effects continue over some period of time? And do they intensify as time goes on, or decrease? Using your conclusions, pick a time frame that makes sense as you think about the total financial effects of your solution and how you might measure them. Take a look at Figure 3.1 to see how Construction Systems worked out a cash analysis for one prospect. The company took every potential cost saving into account and then added a 10 percent productivity gain suggested by the prospect—and they arrived at a huge financial benefit for their prospect. Interestingly, in this case, the savings without the productivity gain actually paid for the product, and the productivity gain was icing on the cake.

This is a good example of how to probe into the details and make a strong financial case. What you are looking for as you work with your prospect, obviously, is the largest number you can reasonably expect her to agree with given the dimensions of her problem. That becomes the base from which you can arrive at the price you can reasonably ask your prospect to pay for your solution.

- **Second**, determine what price will provide your prospect a significant return on her investment. In general, your price should offer at least a two or three times return on the cash she invests, over the time frame you have picked. Most of you who have been using cost-based pricing will find that this provides a significantly higher price point than your current pricing model.
- **Finally**, change your pricing to reflect the value you are bringing to your next prospect.

The success of this focus change in your pricing depends entirely on the success of your change in focus from products to customers. You must be solving critical problems for your prospect, and you must arrive at the first three essential agreements with your prospect. I want to re-emphasize that the only numbers that matter in this whole discussion are the ones that result from your prospect's quantification of his problem. Your role is to help him determine what those numbers are, but you must remember that he will not believe any number you develop by yourself and then present to him. If you have successfully implemented your first change in focus, then this change will be reasonably straightforward to achieve, and all you will have to do is change your price to increase your margins and profits.

Cash Flow Analysis Prepared by Construction Systems					Smith Highway Builders
	Change with Construction Systems	Hours Per Week	Hourly Rate	Monthly Subtotal	Monthly Total
CONSTRUCTION CASH FLOW					
Foreman Paper Management (35 Foremen, 3 hr/wk)	Reduced	105	$30.00	$12,600	
Job Inventory Emergency Replenishment (35 Foremen, 6 hr/wk)	Reduced	140	$30.00	$16,800	
Transport Time (35 Foremen, .75 hr/wk)	Eliminated	26	$30.00	$3,120	
Data Entry	Eliminated	16	$20.00	$1,200	$33,800
SERVICE CASH FLOW					
Foreman Paper Management (22 Foremen, 2 hr/wk)	Reduced	44	$30.00	$5,280	
Data Entry Reviewer Processing (60 hr/wk collectively)	Reduced	60	$30.00	$7,200	
Dispute Mediation due to untimely invoicing (5 approvers, 4 hr/wk)	Reduced	20	$45.00	$3,600	$16,080
GENERAL CASH FLOW					
Supervisor's Time	Reduced	1.6	$50.00	$320	
Inventory Management (57 Foremen, 4 hr/wk)	Reduced	228	$30.00	$27,360	$27,680
STRATEGIC CASH FLOW					
Business Intelligence Reporting	Bottom Line Improved 10%			$460,000	$460,000
Total Monthly Value of the Solution					**$537,560**

Figure 3.1: Pricing Cash Flow Analysis

How to Focus on Your Value

> ### Why "ROI" doesn't work
>
> I want to throw in a word of caution here based on many hard lessons I've learned over the years. It is a significant error in most cases to talk with your prospect about return on investment, or ROI, when you are talking about the financial effects of your solution and the investment she will be making. ROI is a formal concept in many companies and is driven by structured models and requirements for specific "hurdle rates." If you get involved in that discussion with your prospect's CFO, you will significantly lengthen your sales cycle and increase your level of effort. It's much better to talk about cash flow and the effect your solution will have on expenses and revenues and compare that with the investment required for your solution.

How the change in focus helps you generate more profits

The biggest effect of the focus change is that as you continue to focus on quantifying and solving your prospect's problems and on the financial results your solution will provide, you will become more and more a part of your prospect's team. You will build differentiation from your competitors, because you are no longer pitching a product and no longer seen as a salesperson who will do or say anything to get the order. You will be seen as the one provider who has the level of understanding that is necessary for a successful solution to the prospect's problem.

A number of beneficial effects derive from your new ability to price your product for what it's worth.

- **First**, you'll eliminate "feature versus price" comparisons that result in price-driven commodity-purchasing decisions.
- **Second**, your price will be seen as an investment in future results and will stop being an issue to your prospect—in fact, you may find that a prospect will divert money from other projects to buy your product, because of the financial benefits.
- **Finally**, you'll close more deals and make more money on the deals you close, freeing up cash to expand your company.

Case Study:
Johnson Environmental Services focuses on value

You met James Johnson in the Introduction. As we saw, James was reluctant to make the investment in expanding his sales effort, because his company was not generating enough excess cash to make him comfortable about increasing expenses without being very sure he'd get quick returns. He felt as though the company was at a point where he could break out into a larger market, but he couldn't figure out how he would fund the additional investment he'd need. And he very much wanted to take advantage of the economic downturn to position his company to grow quickly in the economic recovery he was sure would follow.

When James and I began talking about how he sold and delivered his services, I was impressed by the very structured processes he had put in place in every part of his business—except sales. He was providing a fixed-price outsourcing service: an environmental engineer visited each customer once a month to ensure that the customer was compliant with all of the relevant environmental, health, and safety regulations. The structure was bringing his customers exceptional value—the service was keeping them out of trouble with OSHA, EPA, and many other regulatory agencies, at a much lower cost than if they had run their compliance activities internally. He had a very loyal customer base and the business was growing about 20 percent a year by selling additional contract services to existing customers. However, he was basing his pricing on the hourly wage he was paying his environmental engineers, so his costs were growing at the same rate as his revenues. He was not able to get any leverage and was not generating the excess cash he needed.

We first went through the exercise of changing his selling focus from pitching his services to concentrating on his prospects' problems. This was a fairly easy change for James, because he was doing all the selling for the company and was able to implement each part of the change very quickly. Once he had accomplished that change in focus, we started work on the change in focus from cost-based to value-based pricing.

We began by quantifying what he thought he was actually saving his customers, both in avoided fines and legal fees and in reduced costs of compliance activities. He discovered that, on average, the financial effect of his services exceeded his price by a factor of at least four. He discussed his findings with several of his existing customers and got agreement from them that these numbers were valid. Armed with the confidence that he now understood how to sell value, James decided to raise the price of his annual service by 75 percent for the next new prospect he encountered.

It worked. James established the value of his service, arrived at the three essential agreements, and worked with his prospect to solve a critical problem and help him accomplish her business goals. Price never became an issue, and the prospect accepted the new price without negotiation. James thinks he will have the same success with other prospects, and now his costs don't ramp up at the same rate as his prices. Because of his recurring revenue model, this price increase will multiply by the number of years he keeps this customer. He has started generating predictable cash flow that he can use to expand the company.

Summary

So now you've changed your focus in three important ways:

- You've changed your focus from your product to your customer, and to solving real problems and helping your customer accomplish his business goals.
- You've changed your focus from "any business is good business" to highly targeted selling, and increased your sales efficiency and effectiveness, reduced your cost of sales, and increased your revenues without increasing your costs.
- And you've changed your pricing focus from cost-based to value-based, which has increased both your revenues and your margins.

Now that you've accomplished these top-level fundamental changes in focus, it's time to move on to Part II, where I'll be talking about practical sales process and strategy. Part I talks a lot about the "why" of small changes. Part II is where you'll learn the "how." And then in Part III, I'll add the "what"—the sales tactics that you'll use to implement your changes.

Part II

Small Changes in Process

Chapter 4

How to Identify Your "Ideal Prospect"

I've now talked about three changes in focus—ways of fundamentally changing how you think about selling. In this Part of the book I'll show you exactly what you have to do to make these changes, step by step. I'm going to begin by showing you how to first define and then find and successfully approach the companies that I will call your "ideal prospects."

Changing focus is harder than it looks

When you began focusing your sales efforts on the markets and companies you defined in Chapter 2, you probably found that it wasn't as easy as it looked. If you're like most small companies, I bet several things are happening:

- You are having trouble finding enough good prospects to sell to.
- You are not sure who you ought to call in the first place.
- You have found that you often can't get an audience with the right people.
- You are having trouble making the time to make the calls.
- And you've found out that you *hate* cold calling.

So, even though the changes in focus looked like a good idea, you're finding that it's difficult to implement them—and because it's difficult to get results, you may not be convinced the changes will actually work if you do implement them.

You need to add processes to your focus changes

Don't give up at this point. Here's why you're having difficulties: You still have to add sales processes to your changed focus—you need to integrate the three changes in focus into a consistent, repeatable sales approach. Put another way, you need a road map to successful sales. Let's look at what's causing this problem, one challenge at a time:

- You are having trouble finding enough prospects, because you don't yet have a precise definition of the companies you are looking for and a plan for finding them.
- You aren't sure who you need to talk with and are having trouble getting through to people, because you don't yet understand exactly what will motivate them to talk with you.
- You're having trouble finding time to make the calls, because you haven't yet developed a plan for how many calls you have to make and incorporated that into your schedule.
- And you hate making cold calls, because everyone hates making cold calls until he begins to have some success in turning them into orders (you'll still hate cold calling, but success will keep you going anyway).

In this chapter, you'll learn how to overcome these difficulties, systematically build a list of high-probability prospective customers, and begin productive conversations with them. I'll show you how to turn your change in focus into a powerful sales process.

The small change in *process*:
Learning to identify your Ideal Prospect

In Chapter 2, you learned how to define your "sweet spot" markets and the companies that are in them. Now it's time to refine that work and develop and adopt specific sales processes that will guide your day-to-day selling. Your market definitions will have resulted in an unwieldy and undifferentiated list of potential customers, so you'll spend some time transforming this list into a set of real prospects. This process change will show you the way out of the dilemma. It's now time to define your ideal prospect within that market and build your ideal prospect profile.

The ideal prospect company profile

Your ideal prospect is a company where you have the greatest chance of successfully selling and installing your product. These are the companies that have the critical problem you can solve and critical accomplishments you can help them achieve. You need to precisely define the characteristics of those companies so that you can focus on only those prospects that are likely to buy. You can then ignore the rest. In Chapter 2, I talked about ways you can think about how to define these companies. Now you need to get more specific about these definitions:

- **Industry segment:** It's time to take one more look at the work you did in Chapter 2 and be more specific about your industry segmentation. You may want to segment differently, or you may decide that other segments would offer greater leverage. In any event, you now must pick only one or two segments to focus on. More than that will dilute your efforts.
- You also need to revisit **company size and ownership:** You will be more successful selling to some sizes of customers than to others. For instance, I like to work with small companies, because they can make decisions quickly, and I can see the results of my work sooner. Other people doing my kind of consulting like the challenge of working with larger

organizations, or need the higher fees available from those companies. Private companies can be very different to work with than public companies. The owners of privately owned companies only spend money on investments they are certain will pay off—because it's ***their*** money they are spending. Public companies tend to be less risk-averse and easier to work with, if you are good at working with their organizational issues. It will be helpful to you to specify the size of company you want to work with—by annual revenue or by number of employees, for example—so that you can easily categorize a prospect. When you decide what your preference is, include it in your ideal prospect profile.

- **Buying process:** Different companies buy differently, and some buying processes will fit you better than others. For instance, you may decide that you don't want to deal with prospects that have a formal, bureaucratic purchasing process, and limit yourself to companies that do business more informally. Or you may see advantages for you in the formal process as you compete for business. You should include this preference as part of your ideal prospect profile.

- **Location or geography:** You may want to have a national or international scope for your business, and that will become an important part of your thinking about your ideal prospect. As a small company, if you target a large geographical area, you must be very precise in other parts of your targeting in order to have a manageable sales challenge. If you want to focus more tightly geographically, you will need to define the geographical area you want to attack. Perhaps it's a region near your headquarters and can be defined as one or more cities or states. Or it could be "within 50 miles of one of 10 major airports." Or perhaps your other criteria mean that your prospective customers are clustered geographically—high-tech companies in Silicon Valley or Boston would be an example. These kinds of geographical considerations will be another part of your ideal prospect profile, and you should define them very specifically.

- **Special elements:** Every industry has some set of special elements, and yours is probably no different. You may be selling only to companies that have already purchased some other company's product that you add to or customize, for instance. Another element might be seasonality, so that the ideal prospect profile must include timing issues about when the prospect is available for you to contact. Or you may have to deal with corporate budget cycles so that the ideal prospect profile needs to include the part of the budget cycle when they are available as a prospect. I'm sure you can think of other special elements that apply to your situation. Include these elements in your ideal prospect profile.

When you have defined and quantified all of these elements, you're ready to write down your ideal prospect definition. Figure 4.1 is Johnson Environmental's ideal prospect profile: You can use it as a model as you complete your own ideal prospect profile. An interesting element of this example is the large number of special elements that are part of the process. James Johnson has come to the conclusion that if one or more of the "trigger events" he's defined are not present, he has a significantly reduced chance of making a sale, and he has decided to only sell to prospects where at least one trigger event is in place. That's worth thinking about as you define your own ideal prospect profile.

Ideal Prospect for Johnson Environmental Services

The ideal prospect will have the following characteristics:

Size: Companies with 30 to 200 employees in one of the following market segments:

- ✓ Manufacturing
  - Machine shop (widget manufacturers)
  - Medical device manufacturers
- ✓ Construction
  - General contractors
  - Home builders
- ✓ Services
  - Property management companies
- ✓ Logistics and warehousing

Geography: Located in Colorado or Utah

Special Elements: Has experienced a "trigger" event such as:

- ✓ A recent OSHA inspection.
- ✓ Inclusion in the OSHA Strategic Target Initiative.
- ✓ Increasing worker's comp expenses.
- ✓ Lost business because of a high insurance mod rate.
- ✓ One or more recent serious injuries.
- ✓ Contractor working onsite was inspected by OSHA.
- ✓ High hazard operations or targeted for OSHA emphasis inspections.
- ✓ Downsizing and layoffs of EHS position, but still need assistance with compliance on a part-time basis.
- ✓ Responsibility for safety and environmental issues placed on someone *or on multiple people* without the time or expertise to manage it effectively.

Buying Process: Top executive is available for a meeting with Johnson Environmental.

Figure 4.1: Ideal Prospect Profile Example

When you've completed your ideal prospect profile, you will probably find that your prospect list has become significantly smaller. That's actually a good thing. One of the biggest contributors to sales problems is the lack of a process to determine what the best sales targets are. Being efficient with your selling time begins with refusing to sell to low-probability targets.

Now you need to take the next step in sales process efficiency—finding the person or people in the target company who are concerned about the critical problem you defined in Chapter 1. Let's call them "ideal contacts."

The ideal contact profile

So far, I've been talking about companies as though they are your only concern. Of course, companies don't buy things—people do. You now need to build a profile of the people working for your target companies who are likely to be experiencing the critical problem you can solve, and who will be most likely to listen to your story and then take action to buy your product. You need to ask yourself several questions as you determine who your ideal contact really is:

- **One or many?** Can one person in your target company make a decision to buy your product, or will more than one person be involved? This will be a function of a number of things, of course. The first is the cost of your product—higher-cost decisions usually require the approval of more than one person. Second is whether your product or solution involves more than one department in the target company. If it does, you will need to identify the contact in each department. Third has to do with your target company's purchasing process—it may require some committee-based decision-making, for instance. So your first task is to determine how your target prospects are likely to make decisions and how many people will be involved. If several people are involved, each will play some role in the company's decision-making process—he may be a Key Decision-Maker; an Approver; or a Recommender or Influencer. Figure 4.2, the Decision-Making Process Diagram, will help you think about how your prospect makes a decision. Figure 4.3 provides a definition of the roles people play in the process.

- **Job function?** You will need to understand what job function is most likely to "own" the critical problem you can solve. That will be the person who will listen to your value proposition. To start out, it's more productive to think about job function than about job title, because titles often don't describe job responsibilities well. Once you understand the function, it's not difficult to find out which job title is responsible for that function in a company.
- **Level?** It's important for you to consider what level of person in your target company will be able to finally commit to buying your product—the Key Decision Maker or the Approver. If you think the president or CEO will ultimately have to sign off on your order, you'll need to factor that into your ideal contact profile.

So fill out a decision-making process diagram for each prospect company. When you have completed this exercise, you will have a very good working definition and profile of those companies you want to target, and you will know who your contacts within those companies must be. Next I'll show you how to build your list of target prospects and contacts in preparation for the actual work of selling to them.

Decision-Making Process Diagram

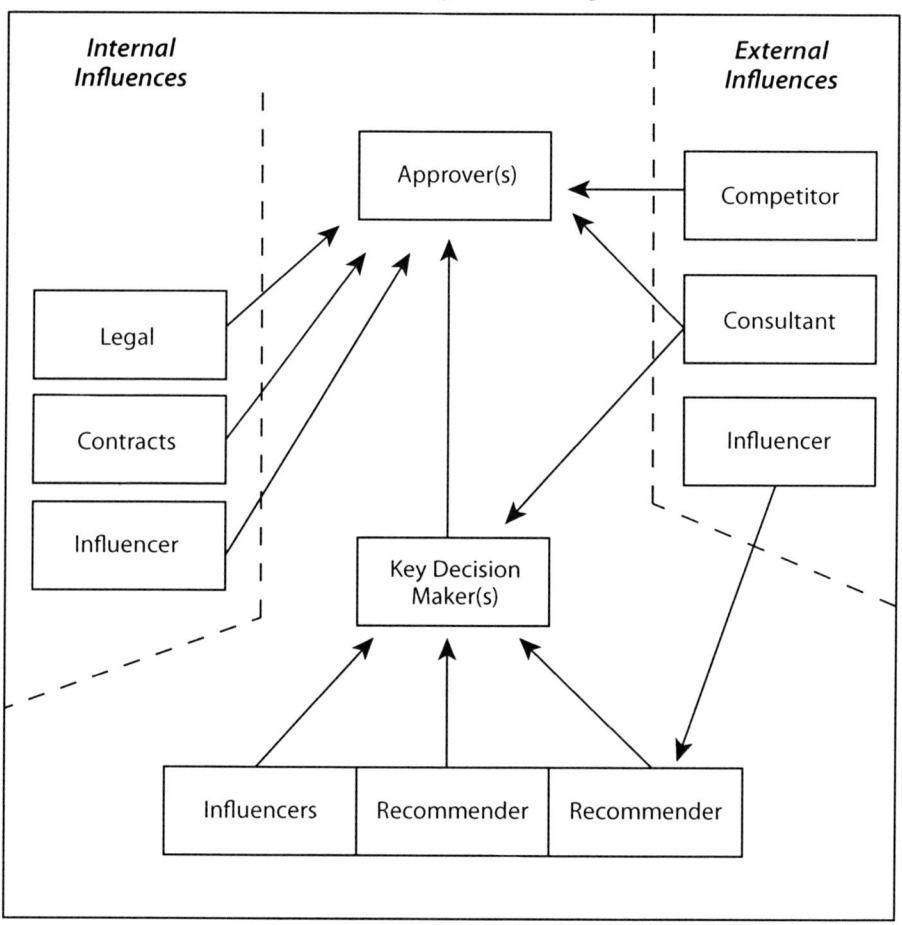

Figure 4.2: The Decision-Making Process

The Decision-Making Process (DMP) Diagram:

The Decision-Making Process diagram in Figure 4.2 is a method of understanding how decisions are made in complex selling situations. Myriad pressures, relationships, and political issues are involved in any complex deal, and it is imperative that the salesperson understands and deals with all of them. Charting the DMP is an essential part of progress through the sales cycle and is incorporated in the Sales Funnel Progress chart for each opportunity.

Each member of the DMP will play one of four roles in the decision.

1. Approver: The final authority over whether money is allocated to this purchase. The "person that signs the check." It is possible that there is more than one approver on an opportunity—for instance, when more than one division of a prospect company is involved in the decision.
2. Key Decision Maker (KDM): The person or people that can say "yes" to a vendor decision and make it stick. In complex sales, there may be several different KDMs—technical, financial, and operational, for example. It is essential to meet all KDMs early in the sales cycle.
3. Recommender: A recommender has a formal role in the DMP. This person might be on an evaluation committee, for instance. Another possibility is that a DMP has given the recommender the task of approving vendors.
4. Influencer: This person has no formal role in the DMP, but through personal or political position is able to affect the decision. There are often influencers such as consultants who don't even work for the prospect company, and there are always internal influencers like legal and contracts managers.

Figure 4.3: Decision-Making Process Explanation

How to Identify Your "Ideal Prospect"

Finding your ideal prospects

Now you know what your targets theoretically look like. Theory isn't going to get you any orders, so now you have to figure out how to find the real companies that fit the profile you've developed—or at least find enough of them to allow you to meet your sales goals. I'm going to suggest several ways to approach this challenge, but in the end, this is where your own creativity will give you the biggest leverage. Some ways to think about finding the real prospects are:

- Think about whether these companies have special characteristics in common that will allow you to easily identify them. For instance, they might all belong to some professional association that you could join—or that would provide you with a list of its members. Or, they might all be customers of a company that would partner with you and provide a customer list. Any relationship like this that allows you to shortcut your search is valuable, and you should think creatively about what these relationships might be in your environment.
- Try a number of Internet searches based on any similarities these companies have. Study the Web sites of the companies you find to decide whether they fit. Keep trying different search criteria until you aren't finding any that fit. This is a time-consuming activity, I know, but doesn't waste time like random cold-calling does. And, as you'll see in the next chapter, you need to do the Web research before you make initial sales calls anyway.
- If you are selling into a limited geographical area, local business journals and their "Book of Lists" are good places to identify companies you are interested in.
- Ask your current customers for references for companies like theirs, associations, or any other suggestions they might have.

Be very specific about what you are looking for when you ask for the referrals, to give your customers all the help you can as they are helping you.

- You can purchase lists of companies that you can sort based on your profile. This is the least efficient way to build your prospect list, but it sometimes is the only way. In the long run, you need to use the Web and social networking tools to build a stream of incoming requests for information. Selling is much easier when your phone is ringing than it is when you are making unsolicited outgoing calls. I'll talk more about this in a later chapter.

At this point, you have a list of companies and potential first contacts in those companies that fit your ideal prospect profile. The final step in this process change is to figure out how to get their attention so you can begin a productive conversation with them.

The initial approach to your ideal contact

The biggest mistake you can make on your initial call to your ideal contact is to try to sell her something. The goal of this first conversation is always to set a time to have a more detailed discussion about the critical problem you can help her solve. Any attempt at sales will only generate sales resistance and make it less likely that you will be able to begin a relationship with your contact and her company. You must develop an "elevator pitch"—a short, succinct statement of who you are and what your company does. It's called an elevator pitch because you should be able to deliver it during a short elevator ride. The goal of the elevator pitch is to elicit a question like, "How do you do that?" In order for that to happen, the elevator pitch must be oriented to the customer's critical problem. An example might be:

How to Identify Your "Ideal Prospect"

"This is John Smith from Acme Widget Corporation. We help our customers deal with the challenge of . . . [insert critical problem]."

Once you have introduced yourself, the purpose of this initial conversation is to establish the existence of the critical problem you can solve, or of an important goal she is having difficulty accomplishing. This requires a well-planned question that will start a conversation. There are a number of ways to introduce this question—a couple of examples of how you could continue might be:

"I don't know if we should be talking or not. If you could tell me how you are dealing with the challenge of . . . [insert the critical problem], we could quickly determine if we should continue the conversation."

Or, simply, "I wonder how you are dealing with this challenge."

You should see any positive answer to these questions as an invitation to request a meeting to conduct a detailed discussion of the problem and how your company might help. As I said at the beginning of this section, the goal of this call is to arrange a meeting with your contact, not to sell. Below is a call script that shows how Johnson Environmental dealt with this issue. It's not a bad idea for you to develop a script of your own.

Johnson Environmental Initial Call Script

If the prospective customer's "trigger event" was OSHA-related—either the company is on the Strategic Targeting Initiative or had a recent inspection . . .

> "Hi, this is _____ . I'm a Principal Consultant with Johnson Environmental. We work with

> *companies like yours and provide a program that guarantees that you are OSHA compliant and also helps you reduce injuries and worker's comp rates. I believe that you are on the OSHA Strategic Targeting Initiative (OR have had a recent OSHA inspection). Is that the case?"*

If you have done your research, you know that the answer will be affirmative. Then...

> *"I'd like to ask you a couple of questions about that—how are you dealing with the OSHA issue?" (Be specific about which issue.)*

You may get many possible answers to this question. The key is to remember that you are not making this call to argue, discuss, or persuade; you're making the call to set a meeting to discuss whether Johnson can help.

So, any answer that states that the contact is having problems with compliance, or their resources are thin, or in any way suggests there is a problem that the contact is worried about gets a response like...

> *"We've been able to help many companies with these kinds of problems. It seems to me that a meeting with James Johnson, our president, would give you and us an opportunity to see if we can help. If you are willing to invest a half hour, I'm sure James will be. Can we schedule a meeting?"*

Voicemail and Gatekeepers

You may have to deal with two other issues as you make these initial calls. The first is that you will often end up in your contact's voice mail; the second is that you may end up talking with a "gatekeeper"—an administrative assistant whose job it is to screen your contact's calls.

When you encounter voice mail, you can either leave, or not leave, a message. I recommend leaving a message, because the alternative is to keep calling until you get lucky and the contact picks up the phone. This used to work, but Caller ID has changed that—people often just won't answer when they don't recognize the caller's number—and you also leave a record of the number of times you call. So the question is, what message do you leave? Again, two choices: You can just leave your name and number, or you can leave a more detailed message. Since just leaving your name and number usually gets you the same reaction that not leaving a message does, I recommend leaving a message consisting of your elevator pitch and a request for a call-back to discuss the question about the critical problem. You will find that this has the greatest success rate, and it also leaves open the possibility of calling again with a slightly different version of the question.

Gatekeepers reward only one approach. You must enlist their help in order ultimately to have the conversation with your contact. The best way to do this is to treat gatekeepers as the potentially important, valuable allies that they are. Remember that they are real people, not just obstacles, and treat them as such. Give them the elevator pitch, telling them that this is what you want to talk with the contact about. Ask them to help you schedule a short initial phone conversation to determine whether there is a reason for further discussion. Just as when you are talking to a contact, remember that the goal is a meeting, not a sale.

How the change in process increases your sales

The primary effect of implementing this change is that your "hit rate" of gaining access to your prospects will be much better.

- **First**, you are calling on prospective customers you are pretty sure have a problem you can help solve, and they will be more receptive to your call. And you will be talking with the person who cares about, and will want to solve, that problem.
- **Second**, you will convert more of these initial calls to meetings, because you are beginning your conversation with a question about an issue that matters to your contact rather than a pitch about your product. This will lower his initial resistance to talking with you. You will become a potential helper in his mind, rather than an irritation, and he will want to continue the conversation to find out how much help you can be.
- **Third**, because you will have more success with your prospecting calls and will be having more in-person meetings, you will be working on more potential deals, and those deals will be better qualified. Having more qualified prospects means more business—that's just basic arithmetic.

In the next chapter, I'll talk about how to manage this wealth of new prospects to maximize the number of deals you close.

Case Study:
Johnson Environmental Services Finds Its Ideal Prospect

I'll use James Johnson again for this example. You remember that his company, Johnson Environmental Services, provides environmental, health, and safety services to manufacturing companies. Most of the Figures in this chapter are from Johnson. When we started working together, James was trying to sell to a broad range of prospects, and he felt the amount of effort required to contact them was overwhelming. The effect was that nobody was making prospecting calls on any regular basis, and no new accounts were being added to the customer base. We decided that in order for this situation to change, he was going to have to define an ideal prospect profile and then figure out how to identify and contact companies with that profile.

He had already completed the exercise about focusing on market segments, and had identified a few manufacturing industry segments that were more likely to have serious problems that Johnson Environmental could solve. James also knew from experience that companies that had recently had OSHA inspections or were targeted by OSHA were really good prospects for his services. I asked how many of these companies were reasonably close geographically, and he wasn't sure. He thought that if he could identify these companies, he might have a good prospecting list.

It turned out to be easy to get the list of companies that had endured OSHA inspections during the past year, but OSHA was unwilling to give James the list of companies that had received letters notifying them that they were OSHA targets. He got creative and submitted a Freedom of Information Act request and immediately received the list. After working through these two lists to eliminate companies that weren't in the ideal industry segments, he ended up with a list of 36 companies that met the ideal prospect profile and had the OSHA difficulties. This was a manageable number.

James built his elevator pitch, along with some responses to likely questions (see the call script example on pages 73–74), and James and his office manager split up the list and began making the prospecting calls. The new process was very successful. Within three weeks they had arranged meetings with seven of the 36 companies, and a month later had closed two new customers.

Summary

You've seen how defining your ideal prospect and identifying the best contact in the prospect company can help you build a manageable number of high-probability prospects, and how the elevator pitch can help you gain access to the people you need to talk with about the critical problems you can solve. I'm now going to turn to another small change in process and show you how to successfully conduct and manage a sales campaign that consistently takes you from that initial contact to a signed contract.

Chapter 5

How to Build Your Sales Process

At this point, you know what your critical value to your customer is, you've spent considerable effort on tightening your prospecting to focus on your highest-probability prospects, and you've developed an initial approach to them that is increasing your success in obtaining that all-important first meeting. Now it's time to talk about how you manage that first meeting and how you progress from that meeting to a sale.

OK, I scheduled the meeting . . . now what?

Now that you are successfully setting initial meetings with the right contacts in the right companies, you're probably dealing with some or all of these challenges:

- You find that you can't predict how your sales efforts will turn out. Sometimes things go really well and sometimes they don't—and you don't think you are doing anything differently with the good ones than you are with the bad ones. Even with all the changes you've made, you find that your sales results on the opportunities you are working on are still unpredictable and unacceptable.
- You work with your prospect, define the problem, and obtain

the three agreements. Then you present your product and your company and demonstrate your product, but you still aren't sure how to move from there to the fourth agreement and a signed contract. It's just difficult and awkward for you to "close" a deal.

- You lose opportunities that you were sure you were going to win. Either a competitor beats you out for the business, or the prospect just doesn't do anything. And it's not clear in either case why you lost—the deal was looking great.
- You find it difficult to keep track of all the opportunities you are working on, particularly those that just sort of "drift along" and don't come to any decision. You're not sure what to do next or how to understand whether you're really making any progress.
- And you can't accurately forecast your sales. You win some, you lose some, and you're not sure which will happen until the very end. And even when you're right about winning, you often are wrong about the timing. This makes it very difficult to predict future cash flows for the business or to plan ahead.

Your sales calls still aren't consistently successful

These challenges are caused by "seat-of-the-pants" selling. What I mean is that your salesperson is reacting to immediate customer situations rather than moving from one step to another in a well-planned sales process. When you're reacting, it's easy to become disorganized and lose track of the path to a contract—and when you lose track, you often make mistakes that keep a deal from happening. It's much better to have a systematic process in place so that you know what you are trying to accomplish at each step—and

How to Build Your Sales Process

so you know when you're off track and what you need to do to get back on track.

Reactive seat-of-the-pants selling also increases the difficulty of arriving at the three agreements with your prospect that I talked about in Chapter 1. As I said then, if you can't reach these agreements, one of two bad things is likely to happen to you: Either you become involved in a competitive battle based mostly on features and price rather than on your unique ability to solve the prospect's problem, or your product is seen as a "nice to have" instead of a "must have" and the prospect decides to take no action at all. In either case you don't get the order. And when you are in this reactive mode, it's often difficult to tell how well things are going—or *not* going—until it's too late.

It is the lack of a systematic sales process that is making it difficult to overcome these challenges. Without a set of steps that enable you to understand what has to happen before you obtain an order for your product, you have no way to measure your progress or to know how well or poorly you are doing as you pursue an opportunity.

This lack of process also means that you probably have no system in place to help you track progress on your individual sales opportunities and provide a view of your overall sales performance. So you are mostly guessing about your sales forecast and have no good way of building any consistent prediction of how your business is doing. It's no surprise that your forecast isn't accurate.

The cumulative effect is that you are less effective than you could be in your sales efforts and have difficulty building a consistent, predictable flow of new revenue and profits. A small change in process can help you fix this problem.

The Small Change in Process:
Building your sales process

Overcoming the challenges I set out at the beginning of this chapter does not require that you become a super-salesperson—it actually doesn't require that you become a salesperson at all. Being successful at moving a sales opportunity from an initial meeting to a signed contract is not "black magic." It is a matter of applying the same management discipline to sales that you are applying to the rest of your business. I'll show you how to design and build a sales process consisting of a systematic, consistent, repeatable set of steps that you follow on each sales opportunity you pursue. Correctly designed, this process will allow you to guide your prospective customer rather than react to him; it will allow you to define and solve critical problems for him rather than be reduced to a price-based competition; it will allow you to work with your prospective customer rather than sell to him; and it will dramatically increase your success rate on the opportunities you pursue. Most importantly, it will help make your prospect see you as a partner rather than an adversary.

Building a consistent sales process

This chapter will show you how to build an "Action-Driven Sales Process." The process will consist of a series of actions that must occur in every sales campaign to maximize your chances of success. Let's start by defining what I mean by an "action." An action is something either the salesperson or the prospect does that moves the sales campaign toward a successful conclusion. Examples might be: "Schedule a meeting with the CEO" or "Obtain agreement that the prospect will evaluate a proposal" or "Demonstrate the product to all key decision-makers." In the action-driven sales process,

How to Build Your Sales Process

the key is that these actions are binary—they either happen or they don't—and can be checked off as you pursue the opportunity. This gives you an objective and easy way to measure how you're doing. Figure 5.3 is a copy of the Construction Systems sales process from Chapter 1. You can use their process as a model of what you are trying to accomplish as you develop the set of actions that will become your sales process.

Building your list of steps

The first step in building your sales process is to develop a list of the steps that you take in your present sales cycle:

- **First**, review the last few sales opportunities you won. For each opportunity, list the steps you took as you went through your sales effort. Provide a lot of detail. It's important to list every contact with the prospective customer, including the type of contact, such as phone, e-mail, or visit; who you talked with; what you discussed or presented; what questions you and your prospect asked; what sales collateral, such as presentations, demonstrations, or brochures, you used; where the meeting occurred; and any other details you think are important.
- **Second**, go through the lists and find the steps that are common to more than one of these opportunities. Rank them in order from the ones that are in the most opportunities to the ones that are in the fewest. You now have the beginnings of a list of events for your sales process.
- **Third**, review the last dozen or so opportunities you lost. Go through the same process you did with those you won—list and rank the steps you took in these sales campaigns.
- **Fourth**, compare your two lists. You are looking for two

things: first, steps that you took when you won that you did not take when you lost; and second, steps you took when you lost that you did not take when you won. You'll also find a set of steps that you took in both cases.

- **Finally**, make one list that contains **all** of the steps that appear only in your winners, **all** of the steps that were in both, and **none** of the steps that appear only in your losers. This is your list of the steps that you must take to maximize your chance of success as you pursue each sales opportunity.

Turning your list into actions

Now that you've built your list of steps, it's time to edit the list into a useful sales process. You need to use your list to create a set of actions that a salesperson can follow and check off as she pursues an opportunity. Here's how to do it:

- **First**, study your list of steps and reorganize them in terms of time—from what happens first in a sales effort to what happens last. This new list is your first effort at a process, logically organized from beginning to end. Figure 5.1 shows the list that Construction Systems developed as they worked on their sales process.
- **Second**, rewrite each step into an action that either your salesperson or your prospect must take. Use action verbs and complete sentences, and be sure each action is binary—so you will know when it is complete and it can be checked off. You shouldn't end up with any ambiguous actions where there can be a result other than "yes" or "no." Each action should also move the opportunity toward a successful conclusion. For example, a list item like "Discussed our products with the CEO," which is binary but doesn't show progress, might end

How to Build Your Sales Process

up being "Obtained CEO's agreement that product features match the prospect's problem." You can see how the steps in the list in Figure 5.1 became actions in Figure 5.2.

- **Finally**, when you've completed converting your list to actions, examine the list of actions to see if you think you've left out anything that you are sure is important to your success. If you have, add it to your list.

---

1. We set a meeting with the CEO.
2. They have an important problem that we think we can solve.
3. Met with the CEO and he understands the problem.
4. We met with several other people and talked about the problem.
5. We talked to them about the money they could save; they liked it.
6. CEO bought into the savings.
7. We showed the CEO how the problem could be solved.
8. We presented our company and product.
9. CEO likes our solution.
10. Everyone else likes our solution.
11. We submitted a proposal.
12. Construction Systems was told we have the business.
13. We signed the contract.
14. We begin implementation.

Figure 5.1: List of Steps

1. Prospect CEO contacted and shows interest in Construction Systems.
2. CEO's agreement obtained about important problem.
3. Obtained CEO's agreement about what he is trying to accomplish.
4. All prospect influencers and recommenders contacted.
5. Problem quantified with CEO and other contacts; cash flow understood.
6. Obtained CEO's agreement about problem quantification and cash flow.
7. Obtained CEO's agreement that solutions are possible.
8. Completed Construction Systems presentation and product demonstration.
9. Construction Systems solution developed; CEO agreement obtained.
10. Problem and solution verified and approved by all contacts.
11. Construction Systems proposal developed and formally presented to CEO and other contacts.
12. Construction Systems formally selected as vendor.
13. Negotiation of terms and conditions completed; signed contract is obtained.
14. Implementation is underway.

Figure 5.2: List of Actions

Turning your actions into a process

As you begin to use your set of actions, you will find that your list is unwieldy and you will have difficulty keeping track of where you are in each of your sales efforts. To make your life easier, you now need to organize these actions into groups that you can use as a shorthand as you think and communicate about your sales opportunities. Here's how.

Analyze your list and look for natural groupings of actions. A good way to think about this is to look for places in your sales effort where you are making decisions about whether to continue pursuing the opportunity. You will often make these decisions to proceed based on additional investments you have to make. For instance, you have been communicating with the prospect over the phone and through e-mail, and now you must make a face-to-face sales call; or you have reached the point where you must develop and submit a proposal, which will require significant effort on your part. Group your action list so that you will have taken the necessary steps before you make these investment decisions. You will probably have three or four groups. An example of these groups might be:

- A group of actions you must take before you are convinced the prospect has a real problem that you can solve.
- A group of actions you take after you are convinced but before you provide a formal presentation or demonstration.
- A group of actions you take from the time you give the presentation or demonstration until you are ready to develop and submit a proposal.
- A group of actions you take as you develop and submit the proposal and move to obtain a contract.

Name the groups. It really doesn't matter what you call them, but some terms I've often used are "Suspect," "Prospect," "Qualified," "Proposal," and "Closing." Figure 5.3, which you also saw in Chapter 1, is Construction Systems' final sales process. Their process has only three stages—yours might have more.

Construction Systems Sales Process Steps

☑	Sales Process Steps	Date Completed
	PROSPECT STAGE:	
☐	Prospect CEO contacted and shows interest in Construction Systems.	_____
☐	CEO's agreement obtained about important problem.	_____
☐	CEO's agreement obtained about what he is trying to accomplish.	_____
☐	All prospect influencers and recommenders contacted.	_____
☐	Problem quantified with CEO and other contacts; ROI understood.	_____
☐	CEO's agreement obtained about problem quantification and ROI.	_____
☐	CEO's agreement obtained that solutions are possible.	_____
	QUALIFIED STAGE:	
☐	Construction Systems presentation and product demonstration completed.	_____
☐	Construction Systems solution developed, CEO agreement obtained.	_____
☐	Problem and solution verified and approved by all contacts.	_____
☐	Construction Systems proposal developed and formally presented to CEO and other contacts.	_____
☐	Construction Systems formally selected as vendor.	_____
	CLOSING STAGE:	
☐	Negotiation of terms and conditions completed; signed contract is obtained.	_____
☐	Implementation is under way.	_____

Figure 5.3: Sales Process Steps

Organizing your sales process

You now have a sales process! You've built a set of actions that you are confident are both necessary AND sufficient to maximize your chances of success in every sales opportunity. You also have a way to talk about where each opportunity is in your process—they are prospects, qualified, or in the proposal stage. You also can group opportunities that are in the same stage to help you build a sales forecast that is understandable.

A nice way to visualize this is to think of a sales "funnel," as shown in Figure 5.4. Opportunities start at in the cloud above the funnel, move into the first stage of the funnel, and move through the funnel as actions are accomplished. You will eliminate opportunities at each stage, because you are always looking for ways to limit your efforts so you are working with your highest-probability prospects.

Now, when you say that an opportunity is "qualified," you know that a set of actions has been accomplished, and that another set of actions remains to be undertaken. This gives you an accurate idea both of the probability of closing this deal, which increases as you move through the process, and a good idea of how long it will take to complete the process and obtain a contract. So, you have a way to determine how well you are doing with each opportunity, and a way to forecast the aggregate of all your opportunities.

There is an old sales saying: "If you are going to lose, lose early." What it means is that you don't want to spend your time on deals that are not going to happen. Your new sales process will help you adhere to this principle—if you can't check off an action after numerous attempts, you should strongly consider abandoning the opportunity and moving on to one that will progress.

There's one more thing to do. Create a spreadsheet that looks like the table in Figure 5.3 for your process. You will make a copy of this spreadsheet for each opportunity, checking off the actions as they occur.

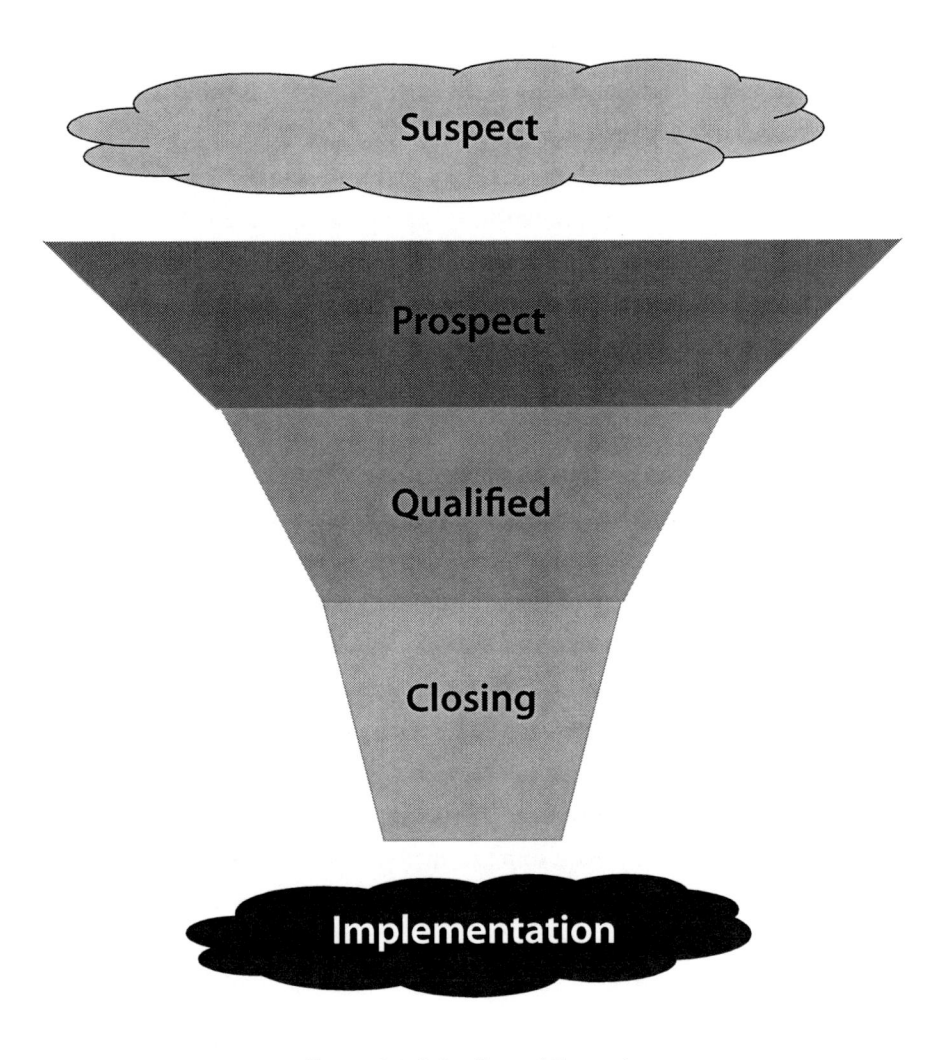

Figure 5.4: Sales Funnel Example

Using and managing your new sales process

Now that you have a sales process in place, your next challenge is to make systematic and consistent use of it. Using the new process must become an integral part of the way your sales force and your company do business—even if the sales force consists of just you! Here is how to ensure that the process is successful:

- Apply discipline to the process. Use the new process on *every* sales opportunity. Salespeople (even if it's just you) will try to convince you that the opportunity they are working on doesn't require the discipline of the process. No matter how convincing their arguments seem, don't allow any exceptions—if you do, you will quickly find that every opportunity becomes an exception, and it won't be long until nobody is using the process at all.

- Manage sales opportunities using the process. *Every* discussion about a sales opportunity should revolve around the sales process checklist. The conversation must be about which actions have been accomplished, which actions the salesperson is having difficulty with on this opportunity, what remains to be accomplished, and who is responsible for the next action. You must refuse to help with or discuss opportunities where the checklist is not being used. This approach will bring consistency to your efforts and will ensure that all parties are adhering to the process. If you maintain this management approach, the checklist and the process will quickly become an integral part of the way your company does business.

- Be open to making changes in the process. If your sales efforts show that an action in the process is unnecessary, eliminate it. If there is an action that needs to be added, add it. This requires that you continually listen to what your salespeople and other employees are saying about the sales process, and that you seriously consider their input. An added benefit is that this helps give them ownership of the process, and will significantly reduce any resistance to its use.

It will take a few months for you and your employees to make this new sales process into a habit and then into standard operating procedure, but it will be worth the effort. Let's look at what you can expect.

How the small change in process puts you in charge

The biggest change will be that you will now be in control of each sales opportunity at each step in the sales process, which is much better than just reacting to your prospect. You will understand where you are in the sales process, where you have been, and where you are going. More importantly, if the opportunity gets off track, you will know in time to do something to correct the situation. An added benefit is that your prospects will see you as more professional and will respond positively to your approach.

The result is more sales. You will close a higher percentage of the opportunities you pursue, and you will eliminate bad opportunities earlier in your sales cycle. You and your sales force will be much more efficient in your use of selling time, and that, of course, makes you more effective. Your sales cycles will shorten, because you will eliminate time-wasting activities that don't contribute to the progress of the sale.

You will be able to forecast your sales more accurately, because the process helps you understand what is going on with the opportunities you are pursuing, how likely they are to turn into contracts, and how long that is going to take. You will also have a much better handle on how your business is doing and what your cash flow projections should be. As you get experience tracking your opportunities through the stages of the sales cycle, you will also be able to identify problems in the flow of business—whether you need more new opportunities, for example, or whether you are not closing as many proposals as you think you should be—and take very specific corrective action.

Another outcome of this change is that you will become a much better sales manager—even if you're just managing yourself. You will have a systematic, objective way to measure the performance of your salespeople as they work on opportunities, instead of just evaluating them after the fact on the basis of what they sell. You will stop trying to manage by listening to sales anecdotes and will begin managing with real data. You will be able to intervene and assist salespeople at the appropriate times, because you will know what is happening with the opportunities they are working on.

Case Study: Equity CRM builds a sales process

From Chapter 2, you remember Roger Spears of Equity CRM and how we worked together to help him focus on his high-probability prospects. Roger also had several prospects in his sales funnel that he thought were good prospects, but that had been languishing in the funnel for six months or more. He admitted that although the prospects were still interested in his products, he wasn't making progress toward contracts with them. He wanted to figure out which deals he might still be able to close and which ones to move out of the funnel. And he absolutely did not want the new prospects he was finding as he focused on high-probability prospects to get into the same long sales cycles.

As we discussed the problem, it became obvious that Roger had no way to figure out exactly where these prospects were in the sales cycle, and what needed to happen to move them toward a contract. It was also obvious that if he didn't change something, the same problem would occur with his new prospects. We decided that he needed to develop a consistent sales process that would enable him to manage these opportunities and take control of how they progressed.

When he analyzed his successes and failures, he determined that there was a sequence of prospect meetings that produced good results, and that skipping any of these meetings significantly reduced the probability of success. Roger defined each meeting in detail so that each had a list of required attendees and a set agenda. He built a sales process around these meetings, with actions based on what had to happen before and during each one. The process naturally grouped into stages based on the actions and the meetings. You can see Roger's process in Figure 5.5, with the meetings in boldface type.

Roger began using this sales process as he worked with his new prospects, and he saw two immediate results. First, he found out very quickly which of the new prospects was not likely to buy—those prospects were unwilling to schedule and attend one or more of the necessary meetings. Second, the prospects who were willing to schedule the meetings were moving through the sales cycle fairly quickly, and not ending up in the "no movement" status of his older prospects. It turned out that most of his sales cycles were 120 days or shorter, once he began using the new process. Roger had a high success ratio with these new prospects, closing 70 percent of those that he brought through his meeting sequence.

Once Roger had the new sales process in place, he decided to use it with his old prospects as well. After evaluating each of the old

Equity CRM Funnel Progress Chart

Opportunity Name: _____

Funnel Phase	Action	Date
Suspect	Prospect is on the Equity CRM Target List. Research completed and Initial contact identified. **"5-minute" conversation** with initial contact completed. Interest confirmed and **"30-minute" meeting** scheduled.	_____ _____ _____ _____
Prospect	**"30-minute" meeting** completed. Current situation understood, problem existence confirmed. Decision-Making Process (DMP) charted and key players identified. Potential show-stoppers identified and strategy set for overcoming. Financial impact of problem symptoms identified and quantified. Potential timing of decision identified and is under 90 days. Competition identified and quantified. Ballpark pricing is acceptable to contact. **"½ Day" meeting** scheduled, key players committed to attend.	_____ _____ _____ _____ _____ _____ _____ _____ _____
Qualified	**"½ Day" meeting** completed with key players in attendance. Information from "30-Minute" meeting tested and confirmed. Key Decision-Makers (KDM) identified. Presentation and demo of Equity CRM solution completed. Agreement obtained from key players and KDMs that solution is acceptable. Objections identified and handled. Agreement obtained from key players that pricing is acceptable. Commitment obtained from key players to evaluate proposal and do business. KDMs confirm that order can be obtained within 60 days.	_____ _____ _____ _____ _____ _____ _____ _____ _____
Proposal	Proposal completed, all Equity CRM internal approvals obtained. Proposal formally presented to key players and KDMs. Objections identified and handled, necessary changes in proposal completed. Proposal accepted by KDMs, verbal order is obtained.	_____ _____ _____ _____
Closed	Contract signed by customer. Contract signed by Equity CRM President. Booking package submitted. Contract accepted by Equity CRM. Formal handoff to Equity CRM Consultant completed.	_____ _____ _____ _____ _____

Figure 5.5: Equity CRM Sales Process

prospect sales cycles, I recommended that he start over as though these were new prospects and take them through the sales process from the beginning. This was a very successful exercise. Roger eliminated about half of them from the sales funnel, because they wouldn't schedule the first meeting, and he was able to get the other half re-engaged in the sales process. He saw the same kind of success he had with his new prospects, and, interestingly enough, several of the prospects that he eliminated ultimately returned, went through the process, and ended up doing business.

Summary

I've now talked about changes in focus and in process, and you are at the point where you have a tight group of high-probability prospects to guide through your systematic sales process to a successful conclusion. In Part III, I'll turn to a discussion of the sales tactics you can employ as you work with your prospects and guide them through your sales process.

Part III

Managing the Changes

Chapter 6

How to Use Sales Tactics to Implement Your Process

I spent Part I discussing changes in focus and Part II discussing changes in process. I think I established that you can make small changes in focus and process in order to achieve big changes in sales and profits. In Part III, I'm going to change gears and talk about specific sales tactics and about how to manage your new process. I'll begin by discussing the sales tactics you can adopt as you implement these changes.

The challenge in this chapter is to answer the question, "What do I actually do as I work my way through the actions in my sales process?" In other words, what actually happens in the various meetings, sales calls, and other contacts with your prospects? How do you conduct yourself to maximize the effect of each meeting? Looking at specific sales tactics and how you can apply them will give you the answer.

Sales tactics: partnerships, not manipulation

When I talk about sales tactics, I am not talking about manipulative sales tricks or approaches. Instead, this is a discussion of the best ways to achieve a partnership with your prospect that will help her buy and implement the best solution possible. In order to be consistently successful in the sales part of your business, you must always be focused on what is best for your prospect, rather than what is best for you. This means that you must be willing to walk away if you can't help the prospect. If you are willing to walk away, you will build a reputation and a following that will bring you long-term success. If you aren't, you will find that your deals become tough to close and that you'll struggle to build any momentum in your marketplace. So, as I talk about tactics, keep in mind that you must be committed to conducting yourself in a way that maximizes your success by maximizing your prospect's success.

The Secret? Don't pitch products, ask questions

All salespeople are looking for the easiest way to close a deal. The easiest way seems to be to spend your selling time presenting your company and demonstrating your products to the prospect. However, when you think about it, what you are doing is hoping that the prospect will pick something that she finds compelling out of all this noise and then buy the product. Essentially, you're betting that if you are persistent, the prospect will finally give up, give in, and buy. This is a lot like speaking loudly and slowly to someone who doesn't speak English, in the hope they will understand. As I've said before in this book, the problem with this approach is that it only works when the prospect has been trying to find a solution like yours and you show up at exactly the right time. For everyone else, your sales pitches result in sales resistance—you're not helping, you're just irritating people. Instead of moving closer to a contract with each pitch, demonstration, and presentation, you are actually lowering your probability of success. You are creating a contest with

How to Use Sales Tactics to Implement Your Process 103

your prospect—you're saying she needs your solution, and she's saying she doesn't have a problem—and you're going to lose.

Let's review the *four agreements* from Chapter 1:

- An agreement with the prospect that she has a problem that is important enough to need solving immediately so that she can accomplish some critical objective.
- An agreement with the prospect that not solving this problem has costs associated with it that are large enough to justify paying for a solution.
- An agreement that there might be a solution or solutions to her problem.
- And finally, an agreement that your product or service is an acceptable solution.

Your sales tactics must be focused on arriving at these agreements—because without the agreements, you have very little chance of reaching a successful conclusion and obtaining a contract. You need to have a consistent way of either arriving at these agreements or quickly discovering that you're not going to obtain them, so you can go on to the next prospect. What these sales tactics involve is asking questions instead of presenting, pitching, and demonstrating.

You must concentrate on asking questions, because your prospect doesn't believe your sales pitch. She has no interest in a solution to a problem she doesn't think is that important. You haven't spent any time understanding her issues, so you haven't earned the right to talk about solutions. You appear self-serving and not really concerned about her situation or problems.

There's an art to asking good questions. If you want to really understand how to ask effective questions, I highly recommend reading *SPIN® Selling*, by Neil Rackham. There are two important reasons for you to read this book: First, it is the best explanation I've seen of the why and how of asking questions; and second, Rackham's organization and description of what kind of questions to ask really works in real sales situations. If you like *SPIN® Selling*, you can continue with *The SPIN® Selling Fieldbook*, also by Rackham, for a set of exercises that will help you develop your own specific questions. In this chapter, I introduce a modified version of *SPIN®* that will get you started on asking the right kind of questions. Then I've added my own set of five fundamental rules about how to ask your questions.

How to ask your questions: a short version of *SPIN®*

Neil Rackham described some general categories of questions that you must ask in order to be helpful to your prospect. As you consider them, remember that you are engaging in a conversation, not conducting an interrogation. Here are the categories of questions you will be asking:

- **Questions to help you find out what's happening in your prospect's company.** You need to understand your prospect's current situation before you can begin to help. Many of these questions can be answered with pre-meeting research on the Web, and then confirmed in the meeting. This pre-meeting research is essential, because it's always a mistake to ask questions when you should already know the answers. On the other hand, it's absolutely OK to verify that something you learned is true, and to ask about the effect of what you learned. You need to be sure that you are not making erroneous assumptions about the situation in your prospect's company—assumptions that will lead you to lose business.

- **Questions to uncover your prospect's problems and to discover what your prospect is trying to accomplish.** These questions are a natural extension of your questions about what's happening. As we have discussed, there are no solutions without problems, so you must find out what the problems are. Asking these questions is essential to obtaining the first agreement. Your questions should be specific, not general. This will be easy if you have done your pre-meeting research about what kind of general problems this industry segment is experiencing and about the challenges your prospect is facing. This will help you stay away from superficial questions like, "What kind of problems are you experiencing?" and to ask specific questions like, "What are you doing about the turnover you are experiencing?" You are looking for a problem that is important and that your contact is seriously concerned about. You may have to ask a number of questions before you identify an important problem. Your questions about the situation will lead you to these questions—if you reach a dead end in asking about a problem, go back to questions about the situation and try to find another road. Remember, you are looking for agreement that there is a problem that is important enough to spend time and money solving.
- **Questions to illuminate the importance of the problem.** These are questions to ask when you have identified one or more problems and reached agreement with your prospect that at least one of them is important enough to warrant spending time and money to solve. You now need to quantify what will happen if the problem is not solved. There will usually be a number of effects, and not all of them will be affecting your contact. You need to assess the severity of each

of these effects, and then help your prospect arrive at a cost associated with each one. This is very important. You can't be the one who arrives at the cost numbers—your prospect must figure out her own costs. If they are your numbers, the prospect won't believe them, and you will not be able to establish the value of your solution. You must arrive at the second agreement—that a serious cost is associated with not solving the problem—and you must also help your prospect quantify that cost.

- **Questions about the decision-making process.** When you have reached the first two agreements with your initial contact, you've earned the right to ask who else is affected by this problem. Review the work you did on the decision-making process in the last chapter to determine who you might need to talk with. You will ultimately need to meet with each person and go through your questioning sequence, reaching the first two agreements with each participant. In some sales situations, you will only need to work with one contact, but if you are selling complex products or selling to a prospect who makes decisions by committee, you are likely to have to go through this step. It is essential to have all the relevant players signed up to the first two agreements before you go further in your sales process.
- **Questions about solutions.** At this point, you've adequately explored your prospect's problems, and it's time to ask questions that will determine what kind of solution would be acceptable. It's not quite time to present your solution, but it is time for you to determine what kinds of solutions will work and to obtain the third agreement. That agreement is that there is a potential set of solutions to the problem—solutions

that would motivate the prospect to change what he is doing and buy and implement a solution.

How to present your solution

It's been a long, hard road, but it is finally time to present your solution and obtain the fourth agreement. And look what a different environment you've created! Instead of a resistant prospect telling you she doesn't have a problem, you are now helping her to determine how your solution would help her solve her problem and take advantage of the financial benefits you've both agreed are possible. Instead of arguing about price, you are discussing how the investment she is making in your solution will pay off, and how the bad effects of her problem will disappear. You're sitting on the same side of the table as her partner in this endeavor, instead of being seen as an adversary who's trying to take advantage of her. Now, when you present your solution, you can customize your presentations and demonstrations to show exactly how you will help solve her problems, and exactly how she will achieve the benefits.

Five fundamental rules for asking questions

Asking these questions will not be easy for many of you. It may seem intrusive and awkward, for one thing, and it's much easier to stick with what you know—your product, your company, your background. Here are five rules about asking questions that should help you be more comfortable as you work to obtain the four agreements.

- **Rule 1:** Have the curiosity of a five-year old. You know what I mean: "How high is up?" "Why is the sky blue?" Don't be embarrassed to ask about anything you don't know or don't understand. One of the traps salespeople fall into is not asking, because they think they should already know the answer, and then ending up not being aware of an essential piece of information about their prospect's situation or problems. If you are curious about something, ask. Don't be afraid of looking momentarily stupid—looking stupid is a lot better than being uninformed.

- **Rule 2:** Don't assume anything. Ask about everything you think might be important. Your assumptions are very likely to be wrong, and incorrect assumptions almost always lead to lost opportunities. So even if you are very sure about something, check it out before you act on it.
- **Rule 3:** Get the terms defined. When you are selling, you will often encounter words, phrases, or acronyms that are specific to an industry, that you are hearing for the first time, and that you don't understand. You are making a big mistake if you don't ask what they mean, because the meaning might be key to your understanding of everything else that is happening in your prospect's company. If you don't understand, you can't help, and it's unlikely you will be successful in selling your solution.
- **Rule 4:** Keep asking until you understand. Ask yourself, "so what?" as you hear each answer. If you can't answer that internal question, you need to keep asking your prospect to explain or clarify until you can answer it.
- **Rule 5:** Always be looking for the "no" answer. One of the biggest challenges in sales is to get prospects to give you bad news. People don't want to hurt your feelings, and they don't like confrontation—so they won't tell you when you are wasting your time. You need to listen for the clues that tell you that you are not hearing the entire story, and confront that

situation with questions like, "Are you saying that you just don't think this is important enough to act on?" to move the discussion to the issues that are keeping you from being successful. The worst that can happen is really a good thing—you find out early that this isn't a good prospect, and you can stop wasting her time and yours and move on to something else.

Now that you know what kinds of questions you have to ask and the rules for asking them, it's time to learn how to organize the meeting.

How to plan your sales calls

The key to conducting a successful meeting with your prospect at any stage in your sales process is to know what you expect to accomplish. You must have a plan that sets out exactly what will happen in the meeting. A major truth about selling is that you are always working somebody's plan—and if it's not your plan, it must be your customer's plan, a competitor's plan, or maybe some consultant's plan. It's always better to be working your plan instead of someone else's plan. What follows is an outline of the components of a successful sales call plan.

Setting the stage for the call

The most important part of sales call planning is setting the stage for the call. Just as you couldn't put on a play without a set and a script, you can't conduct a sales call without understanding four fundamental elements:

- **First**, your reason for making this sales call. This connects back to your sales process, because every sales call is conducted for only one reason—to accomplish one or more of the actions in your sales process. You are answering the question,

"Why am I making this call?" The answer will be something like, "I am making this sales call to obtain agreement that my prospect has an important problem, and to obtain his definition of that problem."

- **Second**, the reason your prospect is attending the meeting, stated from the prospect's point of view, not yours. You need to understand what benefit your prospect will receive from attending the meeting that will make the meeting worthwhile and that will make him want to continue working with you. Your task is to determine what value you are bringing to the meeting. You should ask yourself, "What's in it for my prospect?" Your answer should be something like, "My prospect will clarify his thinking about the definition and dimensions of an important problem."

- **Third**, what a successful outcome of the meeting will be. This will usually be a restatement of your reason for conducting the meeting, plus a statement of what will happen next. In this example, your statement of the outcome might be, "John will agree that problem X is important enough to seriously evaluate, and we will schedule a meeting to discuss the costs and implications of the problem."

- **Finally**, a list of who will be attending, both from the prospect's company and from yours. You need to know names and titles, of course. You also need to know what role each person is likely to play in the prospect's buying process. Will he be the ultimate decision-maker? Is he a recommender or an influencer? And you need to know how the people feel about you and your company on a continuum from someone who is coaching you on how to be successful, through people who are neutral, to people who are actively trying to ensure that you are not successful. It's key to have the right people in the meeting. It's a waste of time to meet with people who can't commit to the objectives you have set for the call—and it's even worse to discover after the meeting that someone essential to the decision was not there.

Define the current situation

Once you have set the stage for the sales call, you need to determine what you know and don't know about the prospect's situation. This is a key step—it's where you keep yourself from forgetting to cover important details during the call. Make a list of what you know and don't know:

1. I know XYZ Company is experiencing difficulty in making on-time deliveries.
2. I don't know whether my contact is responsible for correcting the problem.
3. I don't know if they are talking to my competitors.
4. I don't know if they have defined and quantified the delivery problem.

And so on, until you have listed all the facts that you either know or don't know. The sales call then becomes a tool for confirming what you know and finding out what you don't know. You also have an outline for the questions you will ask in the meeting.

Sales call objectives

Once you have listed your "knows" and "don't knows" you can write down your list of objectives for the meeting. Each of the items on the previous list will generate one or more objectives.

1. Confirm that XYZ Company is experiencing difficulties in delivery of its products.

2. Determine how many deliveries are late and how late they are.
3. Identify who is responsible for correcting the problem.
4. Determine how urgent solving the problem is.
5. Identify any competitors they are talking to.
6. Quantify the effects of the delivery problem.

Ready for success

You have developed the outline of your sales call, and you are ready to go to work. You understand why you are there; you understand the value that you must provide for your prospect; you know who is attending; you know what your desired outcome is; and you have a step-by-step set of objectives to follow to obtain the desired outcome. Your objectives will then determine the questions you must ask during the call.

You'll be much more successful if you plan every meeting and sales call. Your sales call plan will keep you organized as you conduct the meeting, and your contacts will see you as organized and professional. You will be able to respond to unexpected twists and turns in the meeting, and know how to get back on track. You'll be able to listen, understand, and contribute to the discussion instead of being worried about what happens next. In short, you'll be prepared for success.

What will happen as you implement your sales process

Using these sales tactics will allow you to reap the rewards of all the work you've done so far. As you implement your new sales process using the steps outlined in this chapter, you will:

- Become a valued part of your prospect's team, helping him to overcome challenges and make his business more successful. You will be seen as the expert as you help define, quantify,

How to Use Sales Tactics to Implement Your Process

and solve the problems his company is experiencing, and you will never be seen as a self-serving salesperson.
- Differentiate yourself from your competitors by not focusing on your product but instead on your prospect. You will gain your contact's respect by treating him with respect—by being well-prepared for meetings, asking relevant questions, and keeping the discussion on track.
- Provide better solutions for the prospects that buy and become customers because of your greater depth of understanding of their problems and the deeper relationships you've built in their organizations.
- Increase your revenue and profits by becoming more efficient and effective. You will be qualifying "out" early and only working with prospects who are willing to make the four agreements with you. This will give you a much higher success rate on the sales opportunities you work on and greater control over pricing and margins.

Case Study:
Construction Systems implements its sales process

You'll remember from the example in the Introduction that Construction Systems developed a 10-step sales process that focused on the value they were bringing to their customer. What I didn't talk about at that point was how they implemented the process.

At Construction Systems, Vice President of Sales Pete Jackson and I developed a highly structured set of questions based on the *SPIN® Selling* model. You can see the matrix we came up with in Figure 6.1. The questions moved from the situation to the problem and its cost and implications. Pete committed to use these questions in every sales opportunity, and to not demonstrate or present the product until he had arrived at the first three agreements. He also decided that he would plan every sales call to ensure that he was asking the correct questions, that the right people were attending, and that he understood how he would conduct the call. This approach was very successful, and Pete concluded that a specific series of sales calls was necessary for success. He built sales call plan templates for each of those prospect meetings, and then customized them for each prospect.

As you saw in Chapter 1, the results were spectacular. What was more gratifying was that Construction Systems' prospects changed their view of the company and accepted Pete as a partner in their efforts to become more efficient in their businesses. Both Pete and I were convinced that the change happened because of Construction Systems' small changes—because he was asking questions and trying to understand their businesses, and because he was extremely well organized and helpful, without wasting anyone's time.

Summary

That completes the discussion of the sales tactics that will help you become more effective as you conduct your sales campaigns. In the next chapter, you'll learn about the techniques and tools you can use to manage and automate your new sales process.

Construction Systems SPIN® Matrix

Problem Statement	"We are using a paper-based time card system, and as a result our payroll data are not timely or accurate, and our foremen spend too much time dealing with timecards. It's costing me a lot of time and money, because foremen have to deliver the timecards to the trailer, fax them from Kinko's, or spend their evenings working on them. My foremen are 'making up' timecard info at the end of the week, and I don't even know whether people are really putting in their hours."
Situation Questions	1. Are you using paper time cards? 2. How does your time-card process work? 3. Do you enter materials and equipment usage on the time cards? 4. When is this work done? 5. How often do timecards actually get submitted? 6. How are they submitted? 7. How do you verify that the hours are actually being worked?
Problem Questions	1. How much time do your foremen spend on time card entry and changes? 2. Do you get the data in time to easily get paychecks out on time? 3. Are you able to accurately track material usage by job and phase? 4. Are your foremen waiting until the end of the week to enter timecard information? 5. Do you think you are getting accurate information for job costing? 6. Do you think all the hours reported are actually being worked? 7. Are you experiencing materials shrinkage and tools walking off the job? 8. How do your foremen and supervisors feel about filling out time cards on their own time? 9. How satisfied are you with your current TME entry process?
Implication Questions	1. Do you think the paper time card process is affecting the productivity of your foremen and crews? 2. What's the effect of late time cards on productivity in the field and in the home office? 3. How does inaccurate tracking of materials affect the profitability of a job or phase? 4. How does the "end of the week" entry affect your ability to manage your business? 5. How much do you think you are paying for hours that aren't actually worked? 6. Does it affect morale to have foremen filling out time cards at home? 7. What is it costing in dollars and supervisor/foreman time to get the time cards to the home office? 8. What's the cost of materials "shrinkage" on a job? How about tool loss?
Need Payoff Questions	1. If you could track time and material on a daily basis, would it help you to manage jobs more profitably? 2. Would accurate and timely material tracking help you to reduce shrinkage costs? 3. Would reduction in time card errors help you smooth out your payroll process? 4. Would it help your foremen's productivity to be able to input TME data from a mobile device? 5. Could you increase morale by giving your foremen a way to reduce time card entry time by over 50 percent?

Figure 6.1: Construction Systems SPIN® Matrix

Chapter 7

How to Measure, Track and Manage

In this chapter, you will learn how to manage the changes you've made in your sales organization and your company and how to measure your progress with the new sales process. I'll also discuss the tools you can use for measuring, tracking, and managing sales results and salespeople.

Setting goals for sales

In order to successfully manage salespeople (or even to manage yourself, acting as a salesperson), you must set your overall sales goals, decide what variables you will track to ensure that you meet your goals, and set out objective measurements for those variables. Salespeople will not be motivated by goals that seem unachievable, so it's important to set goals realistically. This is not as simple as it sounds, even at the level of setting your overall goals.

Overall sales goals

The simple way to think about overall sales goals is in terms of orders. The value and timing of the orders that you need to run your business is, of course, based on the revenue or cash that the orders generate. Even though revenues are the lifeblood of your business, setting sales goals for your sales force based on orders is usually easier to manage than setting them based on revenue.

As you set your overall sales goals, it's important that you balance your company's need for revenue against what your sales force can realistically achieve. You must set your goals from both a "top-down" and a "bottom-up" perspective. Your "top-down" perspective considers what level of sales is necessary to make the company successful; your "bottom-up" perspective must deal with what the sales force can deliver.

It's fairly simple to do the top-down analysis. Your company's expense line and expected profit margins will determine your revenue needs. The bottom-up analysis is trickier. You must consider such factors as the average size of a deal, the number of sales calls it takes to close the deal, the average sales cycle time, and the number of sales calls you can expect a salesperson to make in a week. Figure 7.1 provides an example of how you might calculate this bottom-up number. Once you've figured out what is possible for your sales force, you must adjust the "top-down" and "bottom-up" numbers until your overall sales goals make sense from both perspectives. You might adjust your revenue needs, hire additional salespeople, or rethink your bottom-up calculations and assumptions. The important thing to remember is that neither perspective alone will result in goals that you can successfully meet.

Bottom-up Sales Goal Planning Example
The method:

- ✓ Quantify your average deal size.
- ✓ Determine how many sales calls it takes from initial contact to final contract.
- ✓ Figure out how much time each sales call takes. Include the following:
  - The time a salesperson spends in the sales call.
  - The time spent planning the sales call and documenting after the call.
  - The time spent coordinating the call with others in the company.
  - Travel time.
  - Any other call-specific tasks necessary to conduct the sales call, such as presentation or demo preparation.
- ✓ Determine how much time a salesperson spends on other activities each week:
  - Prospecting.
  - Internal meetings, training, etc.
  - Other required non-sales activities.
- ✓ Do the Math: total time available minus non-sales call time equals time available for sales calls. Divide by average sales call time to find the number of sales calls a salesperson can make each week.
- ✓ Determine how many prospects you need to close one deal.

Now you know how many hours per week are available for sales calls, how many calls a sales person must make to close a deal, and how many prospects it takes to close each deal, so you can calculate how many deals a salesperson can do per month, quarter or year. Multiplied by the average deal size, this gives you a rational quota.

> **Bottom-up Sales Goal Planning Example (continued)**
> ***The calculation:***
>
> | | |
> |---|---:|
> | Average deal size | $ 10,000 |
> | # of calls to close an opportunity | 6 |
> | Total call time including planning, etc. | 3 hours |
> | Prospecting time required per week | 8 hours |
> | Other task time required per week | 8 hours |
> | Available selling time per week | 24 hours |
> | Number of sales calls per month (96 hours/3 hours) | 32 |
> | Closing ratio of opportunities | 50 percent |
> | Number of deals per month possible per salesperson | 2.5 |
> | (32 total calls/6 calls per order times 50 percent) | |
> | Annual order value per salesperson ($10,000 x 30) | $ 300,000 |

Figure 7.1: Bottom-up Sales Goal Example

Intermediate sales measurements and objectives

Setting overall sales goals and monitoring them will give you a good start, but you still won't have enough information to intelligently manage your sales operation. If overall goals are all you use, you won't know you have a problem with a sales opportunity soon enough to do anything about it. You need to measure intermediate objectives that will give you some assurance that your sales efforts are progressing toward a successful conclusion. The question is, what else should you measure?

I like to look at two types of intermediate objectives: The first is what I call "activity" objectives, which measure things that happen during the sales cycle. The second is what I call "post-sales

How to Measure, Track and Manage

objectives," which have to do with the quality of the deals you have sold. Different objectives will be useful for different companies; you will probably want to use some combination of the two types in your business.

Examples of activity objectives:

- The number of outgoing calls each salesperson makes per day, or per week. This will give you an early idea of how much effort is going into the top of your sales funnel. It will be a very important activity to measure if you are selling a lot of smaller deals and need a constant flow of new prospects to assure you that you will have enough deals in each selling period. It will not be as critical if you are selling fewer and larger deals, although it will still be important. You need to determine how many calls your sales force needs to make to keep your sales funnel full, and then manage the process to ensure that salespeople are making those calls. You may find that dedicating a person or people to prospecting will be necessary to keep the flow at acceptable levels. As you accumulate data from this measurement, you may also be able to modify your calling process to increase the "hit rate" and to convert more calls to initial meetings.
- The number of initial meetings each salesperson conducts with new prospects. This will give you an early indication of how many qualified prospects will end up in your funnel. Combined with tracking outgoing calls, measuring this activity has the added value of tracking the effectiveness of your outgoing calling. No matter what the size or number of deals, this is an important measurement to make. It lets you know

how many potential new customers your sales force is contacting and gives you an early look at the flow of potential deals.

- The total number of opportunities each salesperson has in the sales funnel. This gives you a measure of overall activity level. The desired level will change, depending on the size of the deals, the sales cycle, and the conversion rates from stage to stage. A good rule of thumb to start with might be to require a salesperson to have deals totaling four times his quota in his sales funnel for any calendar period. For instance, if the salesperson's quota for a calendar quarter is $200,000, at the beginning of any month you would like to see him working on $800,000 worth of sales opportunities that have closing dates during the next three months. You can apply this logic to any period—week, month, or year—and adjust the multiplier up or down as you learn how much potential business is necessary to assure on-quota sales performance.

- The distribution of opportunities in the salesperson's funnel. The funnel should have more opportunities in the early stages than in the late stages, and the number of opportunities in each stage should reflect the conversion rate from that stage to the next. For instance, if half of your proposals get rejected, then you need to have twice as many opportunities in the "Proposal" stage as in the "Closing the Deal" stage. You need to keep the funnel balanced so that there is a steady flow of opportunities from top to bottom. The specific number in each stage will be a function of your unique sales cycle. It also can be good to measure and track the number of days each opportunity has been in its current stage to be sure that your opportunities continue to move toward closing.

- The number of initial discovery meetings, or proposals, or any other important milestone you use, that the salesperson has scheduled. These intermediate milestone objectives ensure that progress is being made on each opportunity and that opportunities are moving through the funnel. You can also report on these objectives to get a picture of how your overall funnel is doing.

Examples of post-sale objectives

Now let's look at the second type: "post-sale objectives." These are useful as indicators of whether your salespeople are working on deals that are good for the company and will contribute to your bottom line. Here are some examples to consider:

- The margins you are obtaining on the business you close. You should have a target for this objective and determine your expected margins on an opportunity before you approve a proposal. Proposal approvals can become part of your sales process and be required for any deal that is not sold at list price with standard terms and conditions.
- Price discounts that you offer prospective customers. It's important to have criteria that define what kinds of sales situations will convince you to offer discounts, so that competitive sales pressure doesn't always drive your pricing decisions. You may want to allow certain kinds of discounts—discounts for high-volume purchases are an example—or give a small discounting permission to salespeople to ease the final price negotiation. The key is that your discounting criteria become part of your standard pricing and that you have calculated the discounted margins and found them acceptable.
- The success of your deliveries/installations/implementations. You need to measure your customer's perception of success

with your product and be sure he has an excellent experience. This is often a function of how expectations have been set during the sales process, and if there are problems, you may need to make changes in your sales process, your delivery process, or both.

Over time, you will be able to decide which of these objectives, or other objectives you have figured out for yourself, provide the information you need to ensure consistent sales success. Continue to use the ones that consistently work for you, and forget about the ones that don't. The important thing is to have specific, measureable goals or you won't be able to manage your sales efforts successfully. You'll end up managing based on sales anecdotes and subjective views of what's going on, instead of managing based on performance versus targets. Managing sales without specific goals is a recipe for failure that you should make every effort to avoid.

Automating the process:
Measuring and tracking sales goals and objectives

Now that you've identified and quantified your objectives, you need to automate the process of systematic measurement, tracking, and reporting of these objectives. Generally speaking, you can use two kinds of automated tools: The first are single-person tools; the second are tools that allow information to be easily shared by a number of people. Your choice should be based on your specific organizational requirements. Here's a look at each kind:

Single-person tools

You can track your objectives with tools such as spreadsheets or Microsoft Outlook, as long as you don't need to share the information in real time with anyone. You can keep track of your contacts, keep records of your meetings, and monitor your sales funnel—if you are the only one who's using the information. You can even e-mail summaries to other people in the company. This tracking method begins to break down as soon as you have more than one person involved in your sales efforts. If you have someone in your office making cold calls to prospects, for example, the spreadsheet approach becomes much more difficult to manage. If you have a salesperson or multiple salespeople, it won't work well at all. You will need to move to a more sophisticated tool.

Customer Relationship Management (CRM) tools

You can use any one of the myriad of automated CRM tools to track your sales efforts. Traditional software tools such as Gold-Mine and ACT were originally developed as contact management systems intended to track sales efforts by managing contacts and companies. Most of these tools have been expanded and now offer wider CRM capabilities, such as marketing campaign management and customer service management.

Other tools like Siebel Systems and Microsoft CRM were developed as full-featured CRM tools and are marketed to companies with large sales forces and complex selling environments.

A common element of these CRM solutions is that in order to use them you must have the ability to manage the server and database internally. These products provide software that you must install on your own server. You must also manage the interface to other software you use, such as Microsoft Office and Outlook.

Even the least sophisticated of these tools is a significant step up from using spreadsheets or Outlook and will provide opportunity and calendar management capabilities, enable you to set up tasks to be performed, and generally provide an adequate solution.

Web-based CRM tools

A new wave of CRM systems is Internet-based and sold on a "Software as a Service" (SaaS) basis. These products are accessed through the World Wide Web; some are free of charge, and some are licensed on a per-user basis. The good ones have functionality that is equal to or better than the software tools previously mentioned. For small companies with limited resources, these systems have many advantages over traditional software systems:

- They are "real-time"—that is, when you access data in the system it always reflects all inputs made up until the moment you access it, without requiring synchronization with a server system.
- They don't require you to install and maintain a server system for the software or to manage the interfaces to other software you are using.
- The software is always up to date—the latest upgrades and fixes are automatically installed and available to you.
- Your data are automatically backed up on a regular basis.
- Customizations to fit your business are easy to make and don't need to be installed on every computer in the company—they are immediately available to everyone over the Web.
- The same is true of sales and management reports—when you develop and release a new report, it is immediately available to everyone.

I believe these advantages make the SaaS CRM systems the best tracking tools for small businesses. They are easy to implement and use, and don't require much internal resource to maintain. The one that I am most familiar with is Salesforce.com; I've implemented it for many clients, and have been very happy with its ease of customization and use. My experiences can provide you with some suggestions about how to implement and manage these tools.

Setting up your CRM System

Once you've decided which CRM system you will use, you'll need to tailor it to work with your business and your new sales process. This isn't particularly difficult, but needs some thought. Here are four steps to take that will make the CRM you choose a very useful tool:

- **First**, involve everyone who will be using the system as you customize it. A major challenge to the success of CRM systems is users who refuse to adopt the system because they see it as requiring added effort without delivering them any personal benefit. As you set up your system, be sure that your users have a say in how the system will be used.
- **Second**, customize the system to match your sales process and metrics. You want to be sure you are capturing the information you will need for your measurements. For the sales process, a good place to start is to set up the sales funnel stages so that you can organize your opportunity reports by stage. You may need to customize other fields in order to measure the activities you are interested in. One example would be a field with a drop-down menu for "Call Type," which might have values for "Initial Contact," "Discovery Meeting," and so on.
- **Third**, either customize the reports that are provided with the CRM system or build new reports so that you can track your specific measurements. Don't forget to build reports that salespeople and other users can use to help manage their

business—that will encourage them to enthusiastically adopt the new system.
- **Finally**, provide access to the system for everyone in the company who is in any way involved with sales or with customer contacts. If someone is involved in working on proposals, delivering and installing your product, developing new products, or providing customer service, he should be using the CRM system to track his work with customers and to keep up to date on other contacts with the customer. This means buying as many licenses as you need—trying to economize here will make you significantly less effective.

Rolling out your CRM system

Training will be key to a successful CRM implementation. It will be a lot easier if you have had your employees involved in the change process from the beginning—then you will just be rolling out the finished product that has resulted from their work. Training doesn't just involve transferring knowledge—everyone needs to enthusiastically buy into the idea that these changes will result in a better, stronger company and that all of them will be personally better off, as well. People must embrace the new way of doing business, because you can't afford the time and energy required to drag them along. So take as much time as you need to answer all their questions and concerns and to obtain commitment from everyone involved.

Training in the new process and tools should begin with a discussion of the necessity of having a consistent message and value proposition that everyone in the company understands. Everything in the new sales process flows from that idea, and it must become part of the company's everyday business approach. Once you've established this point, you can train everyone on the sales process, and on his individual part in it. Your emphasis needs to be on the idea that every step in the process must be taken on every sales opportunity and everyone with customer contact must adhere to the process. Finally, you can train people on the use of the CRM system and how it fits into the sales process.

Managing sales using the CRM system

You need to apply one cardinal rule to assure yourself of success in the use of your CRM system. You must insist that, "If it's not in the system, it doesn't exist." You have to have good data before you can manage, and that's dependent on timely and accurate data entry by your salespeople and other employees. So you have to discipline yourself to say that nothing happens without up-to-date records in the CRM system—no proposals, no demonstrations, no executive sales calls, no nothing.

The strength of a CRM system is that as you measure and report on the correct variables, you can focus your management time and energy on only those issues that need managing. You will be able to see in your reports what is going well and where the problems are, and you will be able to directly address those specific problems. This is much easier than the traditional sales management approach that revolves around discussing everything that is going on with every opportunity. Being able to talk only about the issues that need your attention will make you and your salespeople much more productive. So use the system and the sales process to consistently and successfully manage the critical issues and to monitor the overall sales operation.

What will happen as you track and measure your sales process?

As you set your goals, decide on your measurements, and track your progress, several very good things will happen:

- You will apply the same kind of organized management skills to your sales efforts that you have been applying to the rest of your business. You will manage objective sales goals and metrics instead of subjective opinions about how sales are going.
- Your sales efforts will be as organized and predictable as the rest of your business.
- You will effectively manage your salespeople, correct sales performance issues before they become problems, reward high performers not only for sales numbers but for meeting intermediate goals, and hire and fire salespeople much more intelligently.
- Communications between salespeople and the rest of the company will be much more accurate and efficient, because everyone will be using the same sales process vocabulary.
- Your sales forecasting will be much better because it will be based on your ability to objectively monitor your sales process.
- And finally, these results will continue to improve as you develop a more complete understanding of your sales measurements and what they mean.

Summary

You now know how to build and manage an organized, systematic, successful sales operation. There's one more important question that needs to be answered—how do you hire, compensate, and retain the kind of salespeople you need to ensure continuing success? That's what I'll cover in Chapter 8.

Chapter 8

How to Hire and Compensate Salespeople

Having good salespeople is the key to having a successful sales force. Many small companies, however, haven't broken the code about how to find, hire, and retain the kind of salespeople they need, and they experience hiring salespeople as very frustrating. In this chapter, you'll learn that the hiring process doesn't have to frustrate you.

Hiring challenges

Companies that are having challenges with managing their sales force are often making one of three errors when they recruit and hire:

- **The "magician" error:** These companies see sales as "black magic"—an occupation that is impossible to figure out or to understand—and because of this, they look for a "magician" to hire. The black magic assumption is false, as you've seen in this book. Sales is just as understandable and manageable as any other business function. When you hire the magician, you just perpetuate your sales problems. Sales magicians don't use repeatable processes, they rely on luck more than skill, and they will not provide you with the sustainable, predictable sales effort you are looking for. You want a sales professional who understands exactly what she is doing, why she is doing it, how to do it the same way over and over again, and how to show other people how to do it.

- **The "Aunt Thelma" error:** These companies hire based on a recommendation from someone they know well ("Aunt Thelma"), who, unfortunately, knows very little about sales. Aunt Thelma knows someone she is sure is the best salesperson in the world, and introduces you to that person. It's almost always a mistake to hire that person, because the recommender has no idea what an outstanding salesperson really looks like. Even a recommender who has some idea about what makes a good salesperson has no idea what you need as part of your sales force. Recommendations can be a good thing, but they are useful only after you've gone through the kind of organized hiring process I describe later in this chapter.

- **The "hire the competition" error:** These companies assume that if their competitor's best salesperson is available, that's the best hire they can make. It is possible this is true, but you can't make that assumption without close examination. The competition's best person is not necessarily a fit for you or your organization, and the competition's selling model may be quite different from yours and may require a different type of person from the one you need. It's also worth thinking about why that person is available if she is doing so well where she is working now. If the competitor is available as a candidate as you're going through your organized hiring process, it's fine to evaluate her and even hire her if she is your best option—but only if she is.

The successful hiring process

You probably won't be surprised when I recommend that you use an organized, systematic hiring process as you recruit and hire salespeople. You need to take several steps before you begin your recruiting process. Following these steps will vastly increase your chances of hiring an exceptional salesperson who fits your business and your requirements.

Job description

Your first task is to write a clear description of your sales job. You need to think carefully about what you really want the new salesperson to do before you can consider what kind of person will be able to do it. The job description has two uses: First, you will use it to help you understand what job you need done; and second, you can use it as a job posting as you recruit. At a minimum, the job description should include:

- The job duties. This will include sales responsibilities, the products to be sold, and any other tasks you expect the salesperson to accomplish. Some of these might have to do with prospecting, the use of your CRM, required reporting, and any product implementation duties you want to assign.
- Where the job will be located and a description of the sales territory. This section should also mention any required travel.
- Who the salesperson will report to and who will be reporting to the salesperson, if she will be managing other salespeople.
- Type of compensation. For your internal use, you need to quantify that compensation, but for the purposes of external job postings, just a description of how the job will be

Job Description: Salesperson

Position Description

We are looking for an experienced Salesperson to join the Sales and Marketing team. The ideal candidate will have a successful sales record and experience selling in the manufacturing market.

The Salesperson is responsible for the promotion, sale and account management of the company's products and services. This position represents an outstanding opportunity to make a direct impact on the sales and growth of a vibrant and success-driven organization, and to work in a supportive, team-oriented environment.

Essential Functions

- Create new business and manage existing accounts.
- Cold call new accounts.
- Analyze customer needs and offer appropriate solution.
- Create and deliver sales proposals.
- Qualify, close sales, and manage client relationships.
- Utilize CRM system to manage sales cycles.
- Work with senior management to set strategy and tactical implementation of sales development efforts.
- Perform under a structured sales process with clearly defined goals.
- Actively work to improve the sales process.
- Seek sales training and development opportunities.

Compensation

Base salary based on experience, plus an aggressive commission plan.

Figure 8.1: Job Description Example

compensated (salary, or base salary plus commission, for example) will suffice.
- A description of the company and its products, its market position, and any other factors that will make the job more enticing to potential employees.

The job description describes your best take on what a new salesperson or sales manager will do from day to day and what will make them successful. Figure 8.1 is a sample job description that may be helpful.

When you've completed the job description, you need to decide what characteristics a person needs to have to be able to successfully perform that job. You can then write a set of hiring criteria to apply as you evaluate candidates.

Hiring criteria

Your hiring criteria guide you as you evaluate candidates for the position. They describe the person you want to hire to do the job you have described. There may be characteristics a person must have to be considered, such as a particular level of education and prior experience. Other criteria will be "nice to have," such as specific experience with your CRM system. A list of hiring criteria might include:

- Education requirements: Will a high school education be adequate, or will you require a college degree? This will depend on your industry, and it's important to think about what kind of people your prospects will expect to see representing you, and what kind of people your competitors are hiring.
- Sales experience: How many years of sales experience, and what kind of experience, do you want a candidate to have? I'd recommend that you require several years of comparable sales experience with consistent and provable success.

- Industry knowledge: What level of knowledge of your industry, and your prospect's industries, do you think your salesperson needs to have to be effective in selling your products? Obviously, you'd like to have a combination of sales skills and industry experience, but if your products are not highly technical, I'd make the point that it's easier to teach a good salesperson about the industry than to teach an industry expert how to sell.
- Sales process familiarity: Is the person using a formal sales process, and how is she using it? She doesn't necessarily have to be using a sales process exactly like yours, but because you've committed to using a formal sales process, it's important that she understands the importance of using some formal process and that she will enthusiastically use yours.
- Communication skills: How important is it to you that she is good at written and verbal communication? Clearly, some level of competence is required here, but you may not think that exceptional writing skills mean much in your environment, for instance, and you don't want to require skills you really don't need.
- Computer skills: What computer skills are necessary to be productive in your company? You need to decide what level of expertise in various computer systems a candidate needs to demonstrate. If it's just word processing, spreadsheets, and e-mail, that's one thing; but if the candidate needs to be able to use CAD software, that's another.
- Special expertise: Will the candidate need special expertise to be successful? Salespeople in some selling environments need to have special skills or knowledge to be believable and credible as they work to help a prospect solve problems.

Hiring Criteria: Salesperson

Required Education:
- Bachelor's degree in business or related field, or equivalent work experience.

Required Sales Experience:
- Five or more years of successful sales experience, achieving sales goals each year.
- Three or more years of experience successfully selling enterprise-level product and service solutions.
- Experience working for start-up or early stage company.

Required Sales Skills:
- Understand graphics applications or computing solutions that deal with physical objects.
- Demonstrated ability to use consultative solution selling.
- Proven ability to communicate with and sell to C-level executives.
- Strong presentation and closing capabilities.
- Demonstrated use of formal sales process and CRM system.

Other Required Characteristics:
- Ability to work effectively in remote office.
- Excellent communication and relationship building skills.
- Self-motivated.
- Team player committed to company success.
- Willingness to travel as necessary.

Figure 8.2: Hiring Criteria Example

Figure 8.2 is a sample set of hiring criteria for the job described in Figure 8.1.

Armed with your job description and hiring criteria, you are now ready to set up a rating system that will help you decide which candidate fits you best.

Candidate rating system

In the end, hiring is subjective, and you'll make a decision based on your gut feelings. Before you get to that point, it is helpful to impose an objective rating system on your evaluation so that you don't make a big error by trusting your gut too early in the process. I'd suggest you build a spreadsheet. Down the left-hand side, list the important characteristics you have developed in your job description and hiring criteria. Some of these are not evident—for instance, if your job description requires 50 percent travel, your rating spreadsheet needs to have a "willing to travel" entry. Figure 8.3 is an example of a rating spreadsheet for you to follow.

Set up a ranking column in your spreadsheet with scores of zero to 10 for each item, and define what the numbers mean for each characteristic. For example, for sales experience, two years might get a "1," and six years an "8." You will expect a successful candidate to score high on all the essential characteristics, but you might be willing to consider lower scores on characteristics that you rate as nice to have, if the candidate has high scores on the essential characteristics.

Then it's simple. As you interview a candidate, you rate her on the criteria. Totaling the points gives you a place to begin your comparative evaluation of candidates. You can then evaluate in terms of your gut feelings: Whether it seems as if she'll fit in, what her work ethic is, and other more subjective criteria that are hard to measure.

Candidate Interviewing Grid

CHARACTERISTIC		SCORE

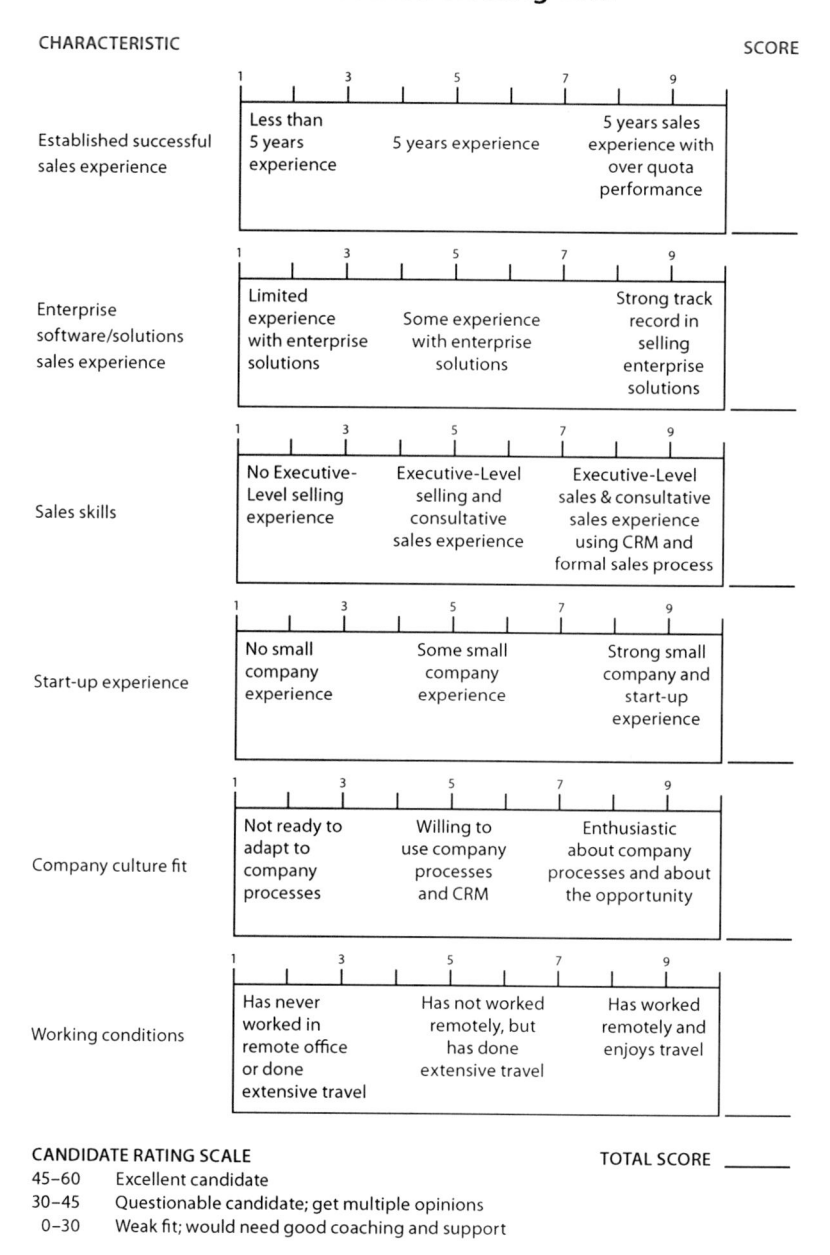

Established successful sales experience
- 1: Less than 5 years experience
- 5: 5 years experience
- 9: 5 years sales experience with over quota performance

Enterprise software/solutions sales experience
- 1: Limited experience with enterprise solutions
- 5: Some experience with enterprise solutions
- 9: Strong track record in selling enterprise solutions

Sales skills
- 1: No Executive-Level selling experience
- 5: Executive-Level selling and consultative sales experience
- 9: Executive-Level sales & consultative sales experience using CRM and formal sales process

Start-up experience
- 1: No small company experience
- 5: Some small company experience
- 9: Strong small company and start-up experience

Company culture fit
- 1: Not ready to adapt to company processes
- 5: Willing to use company processes and CRM
- 9: Enthusiastic about company processes and about the opportunity

Working conditions
- 1: Has never worked in remote office or done extensive travel
- 5: Has not worked remotely, but has done extensive travel
- 9: Has worked remotely and enjoys travel

CANDIDATE RATING SCALE   TOTAL SCORE _____
- 45–60 Excellent candidate
- 30–45 Questionable candidate; get multiple opinions
- 0–30   Weak fit; would need good coaching and support

Figure 8.3: Candidate Rating Example

Finally, you can check her references and convince yourself that you are seeing an accurate picture of the candidate.

A couple of suggestions as you evaluate candidates: Never go against a negative gut feeling. If you don't think the fit is right, or you are uncomfortable with a candidate, you don't need to explore the feeling or justify it. It's enough that you are uncomfortable. Don't make the hire, even if this is your only candidate. On the other hand, if more than one candidate fits the objective criteria, and you have a really good gut feeling about one of them, go ahead and make the hire.

Recruiting salespeople

Now you're ready to start looking for candidates. You've defined the job, figured out what the ideal candidate would look like, and decided how you'll evaluate the candidates. All you need are some people to evaluate. Here are some likely sources of good sales candidates for you to consider:

- Management recruiters. Look for recruiters who specialize in salespeople. The upside is that they will provide you with a list of candidates who are interested in the position. The good recruiters will do a search for candidates that fit your job description and hiring criteria. The downside is that they are expensive and some of them just recycle candidates they already know, rather than going out and finding people who really fit. If you are going to use a recruiter, be sure you find one of the good ones.
- "Aunt Thelma." Now it's time to go talk to Aunt Thelma and everyone else you know and let them know you are looking— and what kind of person you are looking for. You'll be able to

determine quickly if a candidate fits, so this isn't the high-risk strategy it was before you built your job description and hiring criteria.
- Job boards. You can post the job on various job boards on the Web like Linked In or Craigslist. You'll get a lot of action, so be ready to sort resumes.
- Current customers. Ask your current customers about people who are selling to them who would be a good fit for you.
- Professional contacts. This is an extension of Aunt Thelma, except that you are likely to get better candidates.
- Competitors. Now that you know what you're looking for, call any of your competitors' salespeople who you think might be a fit and see if you can get them interested enough to apply.

These sources should give you a reasonable flow of candidates for your hiring process. Interview and check out these candidates the same way you would any other prospective employee, by:

- Assigning interviewers to candidates and defining what hiring criteria each interviewer will concentrate on.
- Evaluating resumes and either setting appointments or sending a "no fit" letter.
- Conducting the interviews and filling out the ranking sheets.
- Conducting final interviews.
- Checking references.
- Extending the offer.
- Obtaining acceptance and keeping in close contact until the person you hire comes to work.

Congratulations! You have hired a salesperson who will contribute to your success!

Sales Compensation

Sales compensation will usually be some combination of salary and incentive pay. The secret to successful sales compensation is to concentrate on compensating the behavior you want to see. The myth is that salespeople are motivated by money—that is not true. They are motivated by *easy* money. Salespeople are very good at analyzing a compensation plan and figuring out exactly how to maximize their incomes—which, if you think about it, is exactly what you want them to do. However, it means that you need to be just as good at figuring out exactly how much you want to pay for exactly what behavior and performance. You can then build a compensation structure that accomplishes what you want, at the same time your salespeople maximize their income—a win for everyone.

(Good arguments can be made that salary-only compensation for salespeople ensures proper attention to customer issues. I'm not a fan of these systems, but if you are, they are easy to implement—so I'm not going to spend time discussing them here.)

Salary

Let's consider salary first. You want to pay a salary that is competitive, or you won't be able to attract the talent you need, so that's your first consideration. When you research sales salary levels for your industry, you'll find a range that you'll need to be in. Within that range, you want to pick a number that keeps your salespeople hungry, but not panicked. Your incentives won't work if your salespeople are happy just making their salaries, and you won't get the customer-centered behavior you want if they are worried about making their car payments.

Incentives and commissions

When you consider how to pay incentives, you need to think carefully about what you want your salespeople to do. For example, wanting them to sell new deals to new customers is very different than wanting them to manage current customers and increase business in those accounts. Here are some steps to consider as you figure out how you will structure incentive pay:

- First, you need to decide how much you want to pay "at goal." The total income you want to pay when a salesperson meets his sales goal, less his salary, gives you the total incentive number you want to pay. Your total income target will be a function of what the industry is paying and your cost of sales. Doing some simple arithmetic will tell you what your average commission percentage needs to be.
- Now you need to consider *when* you want to pay. You could decide to pay an end-of-year bonus, for instance, or a percentage of every order when the contract is signed. You could split the commissions and pay part on contract signature, and the rest when the customer pays the invoice. You could pay a percentage of monthly subscription fees, if that is how your revenue is recognized. My advice is to keep the payment as close to the sale as possible, consistent with the behavior you want to reward. Incentives work better when they are close to the event that triggers them.
- When you know how much and when you want to pay, you can decide *how* you want to pay. You could pay a flat percentage on all orders, for instance. Or, if you want to reward over-goal performance, you could build commission accelerators

into your plan, so that percentages increase as performance increases. An example might be to pay one commission rate up to 50 percent of the goal, a higher percentage from 50 percent to 100 percent, and then an even higher percentage for over-goal performance. And you can modify that by implementing quarterly or monthly accelerators, rather than annual ones. I believe that simpler is better in incentive plans—you want your salespeople to understand what they need to do to make money—so don't get too tricky with these plans.

- Finally, you need to organize the administrative details—things like which pay periods contain commission payments, what happens if a prospect overlaps two or more sales territories, how you recover commissions if a deal gets canceled, how every part of the plan gets calculated, and what happens when territories change.

What will happen when you hire and compensate systematically

When you set up a systematic hiring and compensation process, you set yourself up for sales success. You also eliminate a tremendous source of management time-wasting and emotional distress. A series of good things happens:

- Your probability of making good sales hires goes up exponentially. You will be building a competent and successful sales team that fits into your company culture and is easy and straightforward to manage.
- You will see consistent and appropriate sales behavior, and you will be predictably achieving your sales goals.

- You will be paying appropriately and within your budget, and your compensation plan will help you retain your high-performing salespeople.

Summary

That's it. I've talked about how make the small changes in focus, process, and management that will generate big changes in your sales, and I've shown you the steps to take to implement those changes. I'm not quite finished, though. In part IV, I have some closing thoughts and some suggested books and blogs for you to look at as you continue down this road.

Part IV

Closing Thoughts and Some Resources

Chapter 9

Closing Thoughts

If you are one of the people who have actually tried some of my suggestions as you read the book, congratulations! But if you're like me, you probably read the whole book without trying any of the ideas—I mean, why would you, before you saw how the whole thing turned out? Now you may be thinking something like, "Well, yeah, small changes—but a lot of them, and I don't see how I can implement all of this."

You have a point. The changes do add up, and I understand that implementing the whole thing looks daunting. So you have a couple of options: Either put the book on the shelf for now and get on with your life and your business, or start trying these ideas and see what happens.

If you decide to put the book on the shelf, that's OK. I've done that with books I've read that I thought were pretty good. (I'm going to assume that if you got this far, you at least think there's something worthwhile here.) I've also returned to those books later and tried out some of the ideas to see whether they would work, and if you're not ready to start now, that's what I hope you'll do with this book.

If you've decided you'd like to give my ideas a try, thank you. I have some closing thoughts for you that may help make your efforts easier.

- I've organized the book in what I think is a logical sequence for you to follow as you implement these ideas. That does not mean that you have to try them out in that order. You can pick any one of these chapters and start there—you'll figure out as you go whether earlier ideas are necessary to make the one you've picked work for you.
- So, just start somewhere. If you are at the point of hiring a salesperson, for instance, you're better off writing a job description and hiring criteria now than you would be waiting until you've implemented all of the ideas leading up to that chapter.
- Pick the one idea that makes the most sense to you in your current situation, and implement that one. If you're having trouble getting first meetings with prospects, you may want to begin with the ideas in Chapter 1 and work on becoming more customer- focused. As I've said, you'll figure out as you go whether you need to include other ideas as part of what you are attempting.
- Start small with your first effort—figure out a way to try it without putting the company on the line. Try it, modify it, and then expand it when you're ready.
- Build on your success. When you obtain good results implementing one idea, try another. Eventually you may actually implement them all.

Your biggest enemies as you try to work with these ideas will be your current workload, and just general inertia. If you want to be successful with these ideas, you need to consistently carve time out

Closing Thoughts 151

of your schedule to work on them. I'd recommend that you schedule time on your calendar every day and give a high priority to protecting that time.

One last word: You *can* do it. I've helped many clients implement one or all of these ideas, and every one of them was able to implement and continue to use them. All it takes is the conviction that it's important and the tenacity to keep after it. The results will be worth it.

Chapter 10

Resources

Selected Books

SPIN® Selling, by Neil Rackham

> This book is about how questioning is better than pitching, and what kinds of questions have the most impact. It's based on a years of research observing actual sales calls and is absolutely essential as the basis for the kind of selling I've talked about in this book.

The SPIN® Selling Fieldbook, by Neil Rackham

> A companion to *SPIN® Selling*, this book has exercises that help you learn how to use the theory covered in that book. It also has exercises that help with figuring out how you bring value to your customers.

What the CEO Wants You to Know, by Ram Charan

> This book was written to help employees of companies understand how their work had an impact on the companies' businesses. It's just as helpful for you, as you think about the value you bring to your customers and how they perceive it.

Mastering the Complex Sale, by Jeff Thull

> This book is about selling leading-edge high-tech products

and services, but even if you're not in that business, the discussion of the agreements you must reach with your prospects is worth reading.

Inbound Marketing, by Brian Halligan and Darmesh Shah

This book is a great discussion about how you can use Google, social marketing tools like Facebook, and blogs to generate leads and new business. A "must-read" as we move into an Internet-dependent world.

Slideology, by Nancy Duarte

We all have to do PowerPoint presentations at some point. This book will help you do good ones.

The Dip, by Seth Godin

Seth is a marketing guru, really smart. This book is about what to stick with and what to abandon. It's one of many books Seth has written, and they're all worth reading. I picked this one because it will help you stick with the changes you're making.

Confessions of a Public Speaker, by Scott Berkum

All of us that sell eventually have to speak publicly, at least to give a product and company presentation to a prospect. Scott will show you how to speak professionally and have fun while you're doing it.

Selected Blogs

"Small Business Sales Process," by Andy Blackstone
www.blackstoneassoc.com

You'll find my blog here, which has more thoughts about how sales works. It's targeted at high-tech, but it will apply to what you are selling as well.

Resources

"On Startups," by Darmesh Shah

http://onstartups.com

> Yup, same guy who wrote the book. Again, pointed at high-tech, but generally applicable to your business.

"Seth Godin's Blog," by Seth Godin

http://sethgodin.typepad.com

> Yup again, same guy who wrote the book. I read this blog every day, and every day there is something in it that I use in my business or to help a client.

"Fill my Funnel in 30," by Townsend Wardlaw

http://salesbot.blogspot.com

> Townsend is the best guy I know who writes about telesales. His blog is always interesting and often valuable.

You Can Help

I hope that this book is helpful to you as you work with business sales issues. If it is, and you think reading it would be helpful to other people like you, there are a few things you can do that will help them find this book—and, of course, help the book be more successful:

- Recommend the book on your blog, on Facebook, on Twitter, on LinkedIn.
- Write a review on Amazon.com.
- Recommend the book to your business associates, members of your professional organizations, and anyone else you think would benefit.
- See the latest about the book on *www.smallchangesbook.com* and join the blog discussion at *www.blackstoneassoc.com*.

Thanks for your help.

About the Author

Andy Blackstone has more than 35 years experience as a salesperson, sales manager, and small business owner. He is president of Blackstone Associates, where he helps small businesses increase their sales and profits by applying the techniques he writes about in *Small Changes*. He has spent a significant part of his career in high technology and technology-based enterprise-level sales and sales management, including positions as vice president of sales for three different high-tech startups. As a result, he knows exactly what it takes to be successful in sales. He has been an independent consultant for the past 15 years and once owned a sailboat brokerage. His clients range from high-technology startups to traditional manufacturing companies.

Andy has been applying sales process principles to his own work from the beginning of his career and is convinced that salespeople are made, not born, and that a systematic, repeatable process, rather than a great personality, is the key to consistent sales success. He is an accomplished business analyst and teacher. He knows from his own experiences that small businesses often struggle with sales issues, and he has written *Small Changes* to help them win that struggle and achieve ongoing success.

About the Cover

I chose the image on the cover of the book because it suggests that just a small turn can lead one to a special destination. When I was growing up in Wyoming, accompanying my geologist father on summer consulting engagements, we travelled all over the back roads of the state, and there was always some interesting thing to see or find out about around the bend. I think life and business are like that, rewarding exploration and curiosity. I also like the wide-open landscape in the picture, partly because it reminds me of those days, but also because it represents the idea of the boundless opportunity that exists for the small businesses I wrote the book for.